B*LIMIA S*CKS!

PERSONAL WORKBOOK

10 SIMPLE STEPS TO STOP BINGEING & PURGING

Kate Hudson-Hall, Dip. AdvHYP (NSHAP)

ISBN: 978-1-8382381-1-7

"BONUS FREEBIE"

As a huge thank you, I have created a

CALMING MP3 RELAXATION DOWNLOAD

When you feel overwhelmed by life's stresses, this relaxation recording

will help calm and relax you.

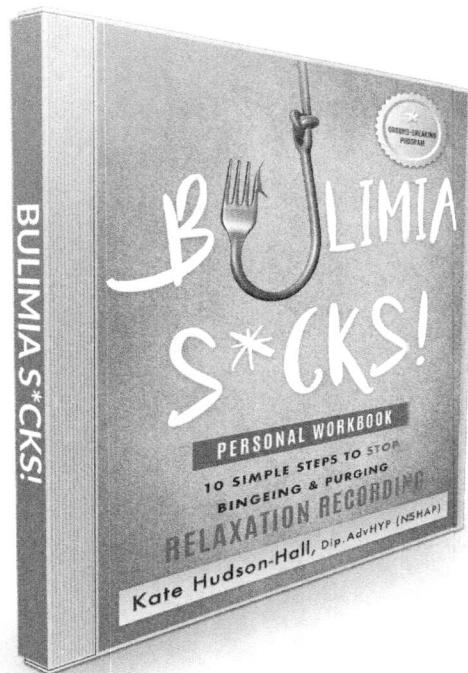

CLICK HERE TO DOWNLOAD:

https://bulimiasucks.com/bulimia-sucks-workbook-relaxation-recording-mp3/

DEDICATION

This book is NOT dedicated to… any leprechauns whatsoever!

This book IS dedicated to Steve. If he could have, he would have, but is still inspiring my rewiring.

"One day
I will be free,

Or,

Day one
Towards your freedom?

You choose."

KATE HUDSON-HALL

CONTENTS

INTRODUCTION

"Courage is one step ahead of fear" COLEMAN YOUNG

HOW TO USE YOUR PERSONAL WORKBOOK
WHAT IS BULIMIA?
TABLE 1: WHAT IF (YOU DON'T)
TABLE 2: WHAT IF (YOU DO)

Your personal Workbook includes incredibly inspiring, powerful tables and new enlightening exercises and learnings to guide you to finally tune into the roots of what's preventing you from taking positive steps to freedom from your Bulimia.

Imagine you're a withering tree and your roots are clogged, muddy congested, and your darn feelings are buried so deep.

In Bulimia Sucks! and now your Personal Workbook, I will be guiding you further into unraveling your debilitating behaviors to change and rearrange them.

Included in your Bulimia Sucks! Personal Workbook are the Bulimia Sucks! tables, techniques, and a multitude of new approaches to reprogram your mind, so it no longer holds you back. Showing you how you're going to begin even further to break through the multitude of negative thoughts, feelings, triggers, and urges. To empower yourself to change your behaviors completely to maintain your ideal weight without starvation and live that happy life you might only dream of right now.

Anyone can develop Bulimia. Bulimia doesn't discriminate according to your shape, size, age, race, ethnicity, gender, or income.

Yes, most eating disorders are much more common in women and girls than in men and boys. Studies had shown that males accounted for roughly 10% of anorexia nervosa and bulimia nervosa eating disorder patients. With today's research, this percentage is much higher; although, statistics may not be accurate, as men tend to be more reluctant to seek help.

Men appear to become bulimic for the same kind of reasons women do, with the added pressure to appear strong, independent, and in control.

So, if you're a man with Bulimia, asking for help isn't a sign of weakness but shows incredible strength and courage. You may feel shame in having Bulimia. But avoiding looking for help could lead to severe, long-term health issues.

Therefore, this Workbook is for all the males out there with Bulimia as well as all the females.

Whether you're a male or a female, with unique productive, insightful new exercises, you can begin to shake off the muddy crusty roots and free yourself from all that's keeping you stuck in your old bulimic patterns, taking one root at a time.

The more profound learnings about yourself, the easier it is to understand how you're going to change positively and nourish your roots. As you learn how you can reprogram your mind, you'll stop bingeing, purging, using laxatives, diuretics, or overexercising.

Plus, you'll address your:

- obsession with food
- fixation on how you look and feel about your body to finally begin to change your life entirely with incredibly powerful tools and techniques.

IS IT TIME TO FIND THAT TRUSTED ROCK TO SUPPORT YOU?

It is hugely beneficial to have someone you trust to help you work through your personal Workbook, to support you as you address complicated feelings at your own pace. This could be your best friend, counselor, pastor, or rabbi.

If you've chosen your bestie, they also can learn about themselves with the techniques to change difficult feelings they may have, not necessarily connected with food but other areas in their lives. So, they too can change their life positively.

HOW TO USE THIS WORKBOOK

This Workbook is to be used either:

- In conjunction with the book, *Bulimia Sucks! 10 Simple Steps to Stop Bingeing & Purging.* It contains bonus tables, exercises, and learnings to work alongside many other techniques within *Bulimia Sucks!* It gives you extra knowledge and learnings to help you take that next step to break free from your Bulimia. If you haven't already grabbed *Bulimia Sucks!*, here's the link to get grabbing: http://www.amazon.com/dp/B08RCPGNQW/
- As a standalone powerful personal workbook with exercises, tables, techniques, and learnings for how you can begin to break your habits and bulimic behavior patterns

I would recommend that you complete all the exercises in this Workbook, methodically taking your time and learning about your behaviors. The more detail you add to each exercise, the more beneficial it will be for you to:

- Really begin to break your negative links, patterns, habits, and behaviors
- Continue learning from your behaviors that may arise and what you can do differently

At the end of the book, there are:

- Links to PDFs of each technique method mentioned throughout the book with specific instructions
- Links to the video demonstrations of techniques mentioned throughout the book with specific instructions for each of the techniques so that you can click straight into action
- Various tables to print out and complete as and when needed

WARNING *IMPORTANT* *WARNING*

Suppose you've been triggered by reading something in your personal Workbook, and you feel like you want to slip back into your negative behaviors. Before you do anything else, I want you to immediately zip to Step 8 and learn the EFT (Emotional Freedom Technique). If you haven't done so already, start tapping on the problematic thoughts and feelings, you have to reduce these.

WARNING *CAUTION* *WARNING*

ICONS

You'll find six icons repeated throughout the book. So, please keep your eyes peeled, as when you see these, it's time to pay attention.

When you see this icon, please think of a positive phrase you can repeat to yourself to inspire your fire and propel your motivation forwards. For example: "I can do this, as I take positive steps toward freedom."

There will be a steaming hot tip for you to think about clearly when you see this icon.

When you see this icon, these are the specific tables to complete from Bulimia Sucks!

When this icon pops up, oh yes, these are for you to reread, think, and absorb what you've learned.

When this icon pops up, you'll find a bonus exercise or table to complete to take you further into learning more about your challenging behaviors.

When you see this icon, it's time to be super proud of yourself. Whether they're small or large steps forward, give yourself the self-praise you so deserve.

"In every day, there are 1,440 minutes.
That means we have 1,440 daily opportunities
To make a positive change" LES BROWN

WHAT IS BULIMIA NERVOSA?

Bulimia is a serious, potentially life-threatening eating disorder. People with Bulimia may secretly binge, eating large amounts of food with a loss of control over the eating, and then purge, trying to get rid of the extra calories in an unhealthy way.

To get rid of calories and prevent weight gain, people with Bulimia may use different methods. For example, you may regularly self-induce vomiting or misuse laxatives, weight-loss supplements, diuretics, or enemas after bingeing. Or you may use other ways to rid yourself of calories and prevent weight gain, such as fasting, strict dieting, or excessive exercise.

If you have Bulimia, you're probably preoccupied with your weight and body shape. You may judge yourself severely and harshly for your self-perceived flaws. Because it's related to self-image and not just about food, Bulimia can be hard to overcome. But effective treatment can help you feel better about yourself, adopt healthier eating patterns, and reverse serious complications. People with Bulimia continue eating within their conditions.

This behavior usually starts with a desire to be thinner. Bingeing on large amounts of food and then purge to rid the body of the food (Mayo Clinic, n.d.).

There are different types of Bulimia; so, let me explain further what they are:

Binge and purge bulimia

This is the most common type of Bulimia in which people often appear to eat regularly or eat a large amount of food over a specific period with a total lack of control during this period of binge eating. Then they force themselves to purge to stop themselves from gaining weight and relieve themselves of food-related anxieties.

Non purging bulimia

Non purging bulimia is when people eat normally or overeat. But rather than purging to compensate for the foods eaten, they will do one or more of these:

- Excessively exercise
- Fast and stop eating for a day or more. (Bulimic fasting and weight-loss fasting have two different psychological and health implications. Dieters focus on food and weight, but with bulimics, it's about so much more. Yes, they focus on their weight and foods, but it's more about achieving a sense of control, numbing uncomfortable feelings, and earning praise or acknowledgment.)
- Abuse laxatives or diuretics

Take laxatives and/or diuretics after a binge in an effort to lose weight and relieve emotional turmoil

Many different emotional, behavioral, and physical symptoms can signal Bulimia

Examples of emotional symptoms are:

- An extreme fear of putting weight on or becoming fat
- Obsession with weight, dieting, and calories
- Poor body image. Seeing themselves as much larger than reality
- Low self-esteem

(People with Bulimia are more likely to be of an average weight for their age group than those with anorexia.)

Examples of physical symptoms are:

- Weight fluctuates dramatically between 5 lbs to 20 lbs per week
- Callouses, sores, or scars on knuckles from regularly vomiting. Broken capillaries from repeated vomiting
- Puffy cheeks. Swollen lymph nodes
- Bloodshot eyes. Cracked lips due to dehydration
- Tooth decay and enamel erosion
- Gastrointestinal problems. Acid reflux

Examples of behavioral changes are:

- Skipping meals
- Not wanting to eat in front of others
- Disappearing to the restroom after meals
- Never-ending worrying about their weight. Restricting calories or eating only certain "safe" foods, usually low calories foods
- Eating to the point of discomfort
- Extreme exercising for long periods, especially after they've eaten
- Being secretive or very focused on food

Reasons why people get Bulimia:

- Abuse
- Negative Body Image
- Body Dysmorphia
- Low Self-Esteem
- Unrealistic Western Culture
- Bullying
- Dieting
- Stress
- Perfectionism
- Family Pressures
- And so many others…

So, if you have Bulimia, the knowledge you'll learn from following the steps in your personal Workbook will empower you to start addressing how you can move forward in your life, free from your eating disorder.

TO CHANGE OR NOT TO CHANGE?
HOW WILL LIFE BE IF YOU DECIDE NOT TO TAKE THAT FIRST STEP?

Let's begin and look at what will happen if you decide you'll not make any powerful positive changes now. I want you to see clearly, even though you probably would prefer not to think about this, but if you do carry on the way you are, where will you end up?

WHAT IF YOU CONTINUE LIVING YOUR LIFE WITH BULIMIA, WHAT WILL LIFE LOOK LIKE FOR YOU?

Please take time out and really think about this. What's life going to look like? Where's this going to lead you in your future?

Answer all the questions in the table if you decide you'll not take any steps toward changing your future. Hang on… there's a big fat reason for completing this table…so read on after you've finished scribbling.

TABLE 1: WHAT IF (YOU DON'T):

WHAT IF:	6 MONTHS FROM NOW?	1 YEAR FROM NOW?	5 YEARS FROM NOW?
• You don't make that decision to begin to change now. What would be the consequences of that decision on your health?			
• What would the consequences of your relationships with your loved ones be like?			
• What would the consequences of your relationship with yourself be like?			
• How do you feel now in your mind and body?			

THE BIG FAT REASON!

So, the reason for thinking and writing down where you'll end up in your future if you make no positive steps to change, will begin to MOTIVATE you unconsciously to start to think about what you can do differently to begin to make gradual changes.

HOW WILL LIFE BE IF YOU DECIDE "YES" I AM GOING TO TAKE THAT FIRST STEP?

What if you decided here and now is the right time to begin to make constructive changes in your life? Visualize how incredibly proud you'll look, feel, and think once you begin on your pathway to recovery, maybe even looking happy from the inside out!

Answer the questions in the table if you decide YOU ARE GOING TO MAKE POSITIVE CHANGES TO YOUR LIFE NOW. Be specific enough that you can see a definite result. This will make it easier for your emotions and mind to begin focusing on how you want to be in the future. This will not only consciously but also unconsciously guide you toward achieving this.

TABLE 2: WHAT IF (YOU DO)

WHAT IF:	6 MONTHS FROM NOW?	1 YEAR FROM NOW?	5 YEARS FROM NOW?
• You have made that decision to begin to change now. What would be the consequences of that decision on your health?			
• What would be the consequences of that decision on your relationships?			
• In your mind and body, how good does this feel?			
• How would you look? What would you be thinking to yourself?			

How exciting life will be when you're entirely free from Bulimia:

- Feeling healthy.
- Your relationships will have hugely benefited.
- You'll be thinking and feeling so positive about your future and you'll look beautiful from the inside out.

"Change may be painful, but nothing is as painful as staying stuck somewhere you don't belong" MANDY HALE

STEP 1

Why Do I Make Myself Sick?

"One of the most dangerous myths surrounding eating disorders is that they are a life sentence"

TABLE 3: FUNCTIONS OR NEEDS OF YOUR BULIMIA
TABLE 4: TIME TO CHANGE
TABLE 5: YOUR OLD FUNCTION/NEED

WHY DO I MAKE MYSELF SICK?

Many factors in a person's life prevent them from stopping their challenging behaviors, and you're now going to begin to learn what has kept you hooked into this destructive behavior. It's breaking down your behavior patterns and reassessing them to learn how you can change them positively.

As you deprive yourself of food, the bingeing and purging cycle begins, the causes and the multitude of feelings connected to these causes are put on hold. As you binge and purge, you provide some sort of fleeting pleasure and instant relief or release, no longer feeling guilty for having the food in your stomach. Some say they're on a high and feel relaxed. Unfortunately, this is only temporary because then the guilt, secrecy, and physical side-effects begin to build up again. The exhausting painful patterns begin all over again. It's like being on a roundabout that's spinning so fast; you can't see a way off, and round and round you go.

If it were that simple just to stop bingeing and purging, then you would have done it already!

THE FIRST STEP IS *AWARENESS* OF HOW AND WHY YOU'RE BEHAVING THIS WAY.

THE FUNCTIONS OR NEEDS OF YOUR BULIMIA.

Let's now look at the function of your Bulimia. By this, I mean the purpose, need, reward, or reason for behaving the way you do.

Once you begin to understand why your Bulimia is serving a function, it becomes much easier for you to know why it's so difficult to stop the patterns of behavior and how you're going to begin to learn to replace this function positively. As you tune into and specifically think about recognizing the possible functions that bingeing and purging serve, read through the list of examples and see if you can identify with any.

Then complete your own list of the reasons why you feel you need to reward yourself by bingeing and purging, taking laxatives or diuretics, or overexercising.

TABLE 3: YOUR FUNCTIONS, OR NEEDS, OF YOUR BULIMIA

EXAMPLES	LIST YOUR FUNCTIONS/NEEDS
It helps me to cope with an enormous number of negative thoughts and feelings	
It's a way to gain relief or some sort of freedom	
It's my only way to gain comfort in my life	
It's the only way I can have any kind of control in my life	
It's a way to relieve boredom	
It's a way to control my weight	
It's a way to distract me from the stress of daily life	
It's a way to punish me for reasons, only I may know	
It's a way to suppress traumatic memories or feelings of anger or anxiety	
It's my way to shout for "Help"	

Excellent, now you can:

- Begin to become aware of your eating triggers, patterns, and habits
- Start to understand your true values and desires. It may be a surprise to learn that your bingeing and purging has many functions or needs, and there are reasons why you're behaving in this way. So, keep adding to this list.

TIME TO CHANGE

Now you have a detailed list of the functions of your Bulimia, let's investigate what positive steps you could take to satisfy these another way and what you can do differently.

Complete your identified functions/needs and what changes you can make.

TABLE 4: TIME TO CHANGE

	YOUR OLD FUNCTIONS/ NEEDS	WHAT YOU CAN DO DIFFERENTLY
	It's time for me	Find other ways to gain time for me, start a journal, read a good book, take a relaxing bath, go for a walk, find a new hobby, or take an online course
1.		
2.		
3.		
4.		
5.		
6.		
7.		
8.		
9.		
10.		

Excellent, having more of an understanding of why you're bingeing and purging will help you to see, think, and feel more clearly about what you could begin to change. Start slowly, make one small change at a time, and keep adding to this list.

LET'S LEARN ABOUT SUBMODALITIES

Learning what submodalities are will give you an incredible tool to help you begin to change how you're thinking and feeling as you work through your personal Workbook.

So, what are submodalities?

Submodalities are the representations of how you view your world. These are the building blocks of how you think, feel, and react to certain things. It's taken from the fantastic therapy called NLP (Neuro Linguist Programming), based on the techniques created by Richard Bandler and John Grinder. You're going to learn to use submodalities to reprogram your unconscious mind to empower yourself to begin to change the way you think and feel.

Submodalities are made up of five different types; corresponding to the five senses:

Visual Submodalities (Pictures)

It's the picture you have in your mind, which could be:

- Is it a movie or a still picture?
- Is it in color or black and white?
- Is it focused or blurred?
- What's the size of the picture?
- Are you in the picture or looking at the picture?

Auditory submodalities (Things you hear)

If you hear a sound in your mind, possible characteristics include:

- Words or sounds
- Tone
- Constant or intermittent
- Loud or quiet
- High or low pitch

Kinesthetic submodalities (Feelings and sensations)

This is your feelings and sensations; they may include:

- Location - where it is in the body
- Shape
- Quality

- Intensity
- Temperature - hot or cold
- Constant or intermittent

Gustatory and Olfactory Submodalities (Taste and Smell)

- Sweet
- Sour
- Aroma – strength
- Bitter
- How strong is the smell?

It's time to put your new submodality learnings into action and discover how to master your mind and harmful behaviors by creating a new healthy self-image and shifting your focus into a new healthier you. So, read on …

"THE NEW YOU" TECHNIQUE

This table is to work alongside "The New You" technique from *Bulimia Sucks!* to motivate you to begin to reprogram your mind to start now to think differently, positively about how you want to be in your future.

Otherwise, zip to the end of this book and download "The New You" technique steps and watch the video demonstration.

Make a list of how you would like to be in the future and then create an image of how you want to be in the future, free from Bulimia. List what you would be doing, feeling, and saying to yourself and then change the submodalities to make this so powerful that it makes you desperately want to run towards it and spring into it.

TABLE 5: "THE NEW YOU" TECHNIQUE

	BE DOING?	FEELING?	SAY TO YOURSELF?	CHANGE THE SUBMODALITIES
For example:	Jumping for joy!	Excited, happy, healthy	"I'm finally happy and living the life I've always dreamed of"	Make the colors brighter and bolder. Make the image life-size. Bring the image closer. Etc
1.				
2.				
3.				
4.				
5.				
6.				
7.				
8.				
9.				
10.				

Keep jumping in and out like a kangaroo, you're reprogramming your unconscious mind, reminding it of the positive direction you want to go in, and it will help you to focus on it.

"Your mind is so powerful, when you fill it with positive thoughts, your life will start to change."

STEP 2

How Do I Stop Making Myself Sick?

*"Even the darn models we see in magazines
wish they too could look like their own images!"*

TABLE 6: IDENTIFY YOUR TRIGGERS
TABLE 7: THE INSTANT TRIGGER CHANGE TECHNIQUE
EXERCISE: AWARENESS OF YOUR FEELINGS AND THOUGHTS

HOW DO I STOP MAKING MYSELF SICK?

If only there was one quick answer to this question! Unfortunately, there isn't, but investigating your draining bulimic cycle patterns and the triggers linked to your specific patterns will guide you toward making a powerful chink in your bulimic cycle.

IDENTIFY YOUR TRIGGERS

Do you know what your triggers are?

Your triggers are the very first thing you do before you fall into that pattern of bingeing and purging, reaching out for laxatives or diuretics, or overexercising. I want you now to think about what your triggers might be. Begin to break down the pattern of what sends you zipping down into that bulimia spiral.

Complete this table in as much detail as possible. Question yourself: What were my thoughts and feelings right before the trigger fired? Identify as much as you can to have a clear understanding of the trigger.

9

TABLE 6: IDENTIFY YOUR TRIGGERS

YOUR TRIGGERS	YOUR THOUGHTS	YOUR FEELINGS	YOUR IMAGES	WHAT CAN YOU DO DIFFERENTLY?
Someone comments how you have put on a little weight	"I am fat and a failure"	Anger, sadness, you feel like hibernating	Image of you looking heavier and standing on the scales	Use the thought-stopping technique. Tap on it with EFT
1.				
2.				
3.				
4.				
5.				
6.				
7.				
8.				
9.				
10.				

Once you have identified your triggers, the next step is to work on how to change your triggers instantly with the "INSTANT TRIGGER CHANGE" TECHNIQUE.

BOOM!

HOW TO CHANGE YOUR TRIGGERS INSTANTLY

This table is to work in conjunction with "THE INSTANT TRIGGER CHANGE" technique table. Otherwise, zip to the end of the book and download "The Instant Trigger Change" technique steps and watch the video demonstration.

In this technique, you'll be replacing the trigger image with an image or movie of yourself engaging in new positive behavior, looking happy and free from your Bulimia. It will allow you to attach the trigger to the thought of you being free from your pattern.

TABLE 7: "THE INSTANT TRIGGER CHANGE" TECHNIQUE

YOUR TRIGGERS	REPLACEMENT IMAGE OR MOVIE
1.	
2.	
3.	
4.	
5.	
6.	
7.	
8.	
9.	
10.	

Can you snigger without your trigger? If not, keep working through all your triggers that spring to the surface and break this pattern as you link this old trigger to a positive new image.

EXERCISE: AWARENESS OF YOUR FEELINGS AND THOUGHTS

Before you move on to step 3, this extra exercise will help you to begin to tune into and understand the feelings your triggers and thoughts created. Take some time to work through these questions to have a clearer understanding of your pattern of feelings.

1. Choose one negative feeling at a time that your triggers caused that sent you into the downward spiral when you completed the identify your triggers table.

Name your negative feeling:

_____

_____

_____

2. Understand that even though it was strong at the time, it comes and goes like waves in the ocean. Tune into that feeling now. Where in the body can you feel it? Ask yourself:

If that feeling had a voice, what would it have been trying to tell you?

_____

_____

_____

3. What can you learn from this feeling?

_____

_____

_____

4. Become aware of how that one feeling distorted your thinking and confused you into believing the thoughts.

Write down how it confused your thinking and led you to feel a certain way that may lead you to binge and purge.

_____

_____

_____

5. List what other feelings then came forward that are connected to this first feeling?

_____   _____

_____   _____

_____   _____

6. Now list what thoughts came forward with the feelings listed?

_____   _____

_____   _____

_____   _____

7. So, what could you do differently when your complicated feelings spring into your body? List everything you could do to change the way you behave when a painful feeling comes up.

_____   _____

_____   _____

_____   _____

It's excellent to become aware of your patterns of events first and then change how you react to these.

"If you can't dig out your motivation, find a bigger spade"
KATE HUDSON-HALL

STEP 3

Why Do I Have This Huge, Overwhelming Urge to Binge?

"Do not go where the path may lead, go instead where there is no path and leave a trail" RALPH WALDO EMERSON

WHY DO I HAVE THIS HUGE OVERWHELMING URGE TO BINGE?

The reason you have this overwhelming urge to binge is that you're restricting your food, but when you stop and provide your body with eating regularly, then the binge urge means nothing = zilch!

Your dieting or depriving yourself of food leads to your cravings. Then, when triggered, in comes your powerful binge voice and agonizing feelings that suddenly explode into your urges to binge and purge. Like an exploding firework, before you know it, there you are with your head in the fridge.

REAL VOICE, YOUR CHOICE

So, what's going to help with your overwhelming urge to binge is tuning into your REAL voice, not that evil leprechaun's.

When was the last time you were aware of your healthy, encouraging voice?

It's time to identify your healthy real voice, which is usually drowned out by that whispering voice in your head, which I liken to a little evil green leprechaun. Others call it "the eating disorders voice" or the "binge voice." Some of my clients benefit from calling him "ED" (eating disorder). But you could call him whatever you like! I preferred an evil leprechaun and imagined him super glued onto my shoulder, hissing viciousness, which then caused my unbearable feelings.

What's YOUR REAL voice?

Your real voice, that positive, healthy part of you, is still there, maybe buried beneath your leprechaun, but if you listen carefully, you'll be able to hear it.

Complete these questions and start now to listen for your real voice with curiosity to help you become more aware of your own voice.

TABLE 8: REAL VOICE, YOUR CHOICE

ASK YOURSELF:	YOUR REAL VOICE:	LIST WHAT IS IT SAYING TO YOU?
Can you hear it in words or sounds?		
What sort of tone does it have?		
Is it a high or low pitch?		
Is it constant or intermittent?		
Which direction does it come from?		
How loud is it? When you hear it, could you make it any louder?		
What happens if you imagine turning up the volume?		

Once you've worked through this list, you'll understand your real voice more, and by connecting with your true self, you can gain back control of your life and begin to recover fully. It's your life, not the toxic leprechaun's!

Throughout each and every day, keep tuning in your healthy voice and turn up the volume, making it as loud as possible or louder!

"Making it real will empower you to heal" KATE HUDSON-HALL

WHAT FEELINGS DOES YOUR LEPRECHAUN IGNITE?

Now you have completed the awareness of feelings and thoughts exercise in Step 2 and started to become aware of how your triggers ignite these feelings.

This table is specifically for what feelings come up when that leprechaun is shouting that drives you to binge and purge? It's essential to tune into all of your feelings, become aware of these, and then learn with the techniques, tables, and exercises to begin to reduce these. Please list all of your feelings that come up and keep adding to them.

TABLE 9: FEELINGS

FOR EXAMPLE:	LIST YOUR OWN FEELINGS
Anxious	
Sad	
Comfort	
Stressed	
Panic	
Lonely	
Ashamed	
Confused	
Scared	

BOOM!

IT'S TIME TO DELVE INTO YOUR URGES

What is an urge?

An urge is an uncontrollable "need" to binge. It's a knowing that if you were to binge and purge briefly, yes, you'll get a reprieve or a moment's break from all the painful thoughts and feelings. It's your way, at that moment, of freeing yourself from all your unbearable feelings.

If you're following your structured eating program (which we'll discuss in Step 4), eating healthily, and giving your body the right amount of the correct healthy nutrients, you will have so much more control of your triggers and urges.

Identifying the specific pattern of your urges can be incredibly empowering. Having a clearer understanding of your urges will give you more control to begin to change. So, answer all of these questions in as much detail as possible and then come back. Keep delving and adding to this list.

TABLE 10: DELVE INTO YOUR URGES

ASK YOURSELF:	LIST YOUR ANSWERS:
WHAT DO YOUR URGES FEEL LIKE TO YOU?	
WHAT PHYSICAL SYMPTOMS DO YOUR URGES CREATE?	
WHEN DO YOUR URGES OCCUR? HOW OFTEN?	
DO THE URGES HAVE A VOICE THAT ENCOURAGES YOU TO BINGE? WHAT DOES THAT VOICE SAY TO YOU?	
DOES THE VOICE OF THE URGE USE PRECISE REASONS TO GET YOU TO BINGE? LIST AS MANY AS YOU CAN?	
WHAT DOES THE VOICE OF THE URGE PROMISE YOU?	
WHAT PAYOFF OR REWARDS DOES IT PROMISE IF YOU FOLLOW THROUGH AND BINGE?	
WRITE DOWN ANYTHING ELSE YOU NOTICE ABOUT YOUR URGES:	

BOOM!

URGE SURFING LEARNINGS (PART 1)

Alan Marlatt, a psychologist and pioneer in alcohol addiction, developed urge surfing from mindfulness. We can learn to take back control over how we react to our urges. They aren't dangerous and won't kill us; they're just feelings.

Urge surfing is sitting with that urge, using your breath and attention to ride the wave out, turning toward it rather than fighting it, going with the sensations you're thinking and feeling and riding them just like a professional surfer rides the waves. So rather than trying to distract yourself from your unbearable urges, ride with them; allow them to be there.

An urge is similar to a wave that sweeps over you. It starts as a ripple in a calm seabed. Then, as it slowly drifts forward, it builds up, becoming bigger and bigger until it finally crashes over onto the seashore then calmly recedes. It continually returns in this never-ending cycle.

We might not have control over the enormous urge or a 15-foot wave right now, but we can learn to surf it, go with it since we do have control over how we react to it.

Work with a less intense urge, to begin with, preferably an urge not related to food, to build up your courage and confidence. List again, in as much detail as you can about this specific urge. Maybe something like looking at social media on your phone or checking an email or text message.

Tune in and make this urge as clear as possible and then see if you can become aware of all the different sensations that come forward and complete the table.

TABLE 11: URGE SURFING LEARNINGS (PART 1)

ASK YOURSELF:	YOUR ANSWERS:
How does it make you feel?	
Where in the body is that feeling?	
How intense is it?	
Does it have a color?	
What thoughts are you having?	
Do you have an image in your mind of the urge?	

Excellent, so when you're ready, let's move on…

BOOM!

URGE SURFING LEARNINGS (PART 2)

When you're ready to start, become aware of where in the body you feel the unbearable urge connected to food and the sensations connected to your urge, and just observe them. As you tune in, make this urge as clear as possible and then see if you can become aware of all the different sensations that come forward and complete the table.

This table is to work in conjunction with the "URGE SURFING" technique table from *Bulimia Sucks!* Otherwise, zip to the end of the book and download "The Instant Trigger Change" technique steps and watch the video demonstration.

This time write in more detail about your urges.

TABLE 12: URGE SURFING LEARNINGS (PART 2)

ASK YOURSELF:	YOUR ANSWERS:
What does it feel like?	
Pressure? Tension?	
Tingly? Warm or cool?	
Where in the body is that feeling?	
How intense is it?	
How big is it?	
Does it move, or is it still?	
Does it have a color?	
What thoughts are you having?	
Do you have an image in your mind of the urge?	
Write down anything else that comes up	

Notice how the urges are like waves. They slowly build, come to a peak, and crash down. Stay with the event for as long as you can. Even though you aren't responding at this moment, you see how the urges lessen and float away. Look at you becoming a real surfer, riding the wave.

BOOM!

"It's not so much where you stand as in what direction you are moving in"

OLIVER WENDELL HOLMES, JR

STEP 4

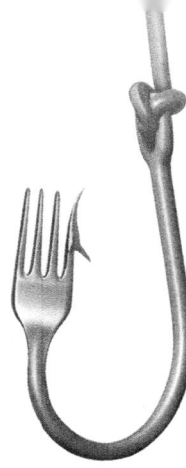

How Do I Eat Like a Normal Person?

"Leaves on the trees grow back even after the bleakest winters. You will too, like a sensational blossoming oak tree" KATE HUDSON-HALL

"When you starve yourself, you're only feeding your leprechaun"

HOW DO I EAT LIKE A NORMAL PERSON?

One of the most important steps you can take to break through your urges to binge and begin to eat like a normal person is to introduce your structured eating program. You can expect a vast 50-80% reduction in your urges to binge by following your plan. Wahooooo! We like that.

The benefits of a structured eating program stretch for at least a mile in length! For example, to:

- Provide your body with the wonderful nutrients it needs
- Undo the damage of malnutrition
- Reduce your urges to binge on food
- Relearn how to eat like a normal person again
- Increase your metabolism; therefore, you'll feel full of energy

OTHER PHYSICAL CHANGES

- Over time, bloating and water retention will lessen, and your weight will stabilize.
- Your throat won't be sore
- No more swollen cheeks, puffy eyes, etc
- You'll start to have regular bowel movements
- Your menstrual cycle will gradually return

EMOTIONAL CHANGES

- Feel less anxious
- Your self-esteem will improve
- Feel so much calmer
- Your confidence will flourish as your social life improves
- Your emotions will stabilize

The list is never-ending, full of so many incredible positives; you'll be like a new you with so much energy.

EXAMPLE: STRUCTURED EATING PROGRAM

The way you're going to start to eat again is with a program that gives you a structure around food and retrains your mind and body to expect food often and regularly.

So, get organized; start to:

- Plan your meals ahead of time. You may want to plan your meals for just a couple of days in advance or maybe the whole week.
- Plan what meals you're going to prepare and buy all the food for the week at one time, reducing the temptation to slip from your positive path.

Adapt your meal plan accordingly, of course, introducing foods you do like!

In the example of the structured eating program, looking at this long list of foods to eat each day, you may be feeling a little too overwhelmed. So, stop what you're doing right now, zip over to step 8 to learn EFT (Emotional Freedom Technique), and start tapping on all the negative feelings that may come up, then keep tap tap tapping. By the end of your recovery, you'll be like a woodpecker, high on life.

Eating healthily is such a significant step forward. It may take time to build up to eating the amount in the chart. So, take it slowly and keep tapping.

EXAMPLE: STRUCTURED EATING PROGRAM

TIME	MONDAY	TUESDAY	WEDNESDAY	THURSDAY	FRIDAY	SATURDAY	SUNDAY
7.30 AM	Lemon water, banana, ½ cup or one serving cereal, 1 cup milk (dairy, soy, almond, etc.)	Tea, 2 slices toast with butter and spread of your choice	Coffee, ½ cup or one serving cereal, 1 cup milk (dairy, soy, almond, etc.)	1 glass of O.J.,1/2 cup or one serving of porridge with milk and sugar	Coffee, 2 slices toast with jam and peanut butter	Coffee, 2 slices of bacon and 2 eggs with an English muffin	1 glass of grapefruit juice. 1 bagel with butter and cream cheese
11 AM	Cookie	A handful of dried fruit	Fruit	A handful of nuts/seeds	Cookie	Granola bar	1 piece of fruit
1 PM	Chicken sandwich on 2 slices of wholewheat bread with butter. Celery sticks	Cheese toastie with grilled veggies, carrot sticks	Tuna salad with a whole wheat bread roll. Dried fruits	Soup of your choice. Whole wheat bread roll. Carrot sticks	Ham & cheese whole wheat bread sandwich. Pickle	Pasta salad with ham. 1 piece of fruit	Bacon and egg sandwich with butter. Dried fruit
4 PM	Cookie	2 crackers with butter	A handful of pretzels	Granola bar	A handful of nuts or seeds	A handful of popcorn	A handful of dried fruit
7 PM	Grilled chicken, ½ cup sweet potato, ½ cup broccoli	Steak, with fries & salad	Spaghetti Bolognese with salad	Pasta with sauce, ½ cup grilled courgettes	Grilled fish, ½ cup potato, ½ cup spinach	Cheeseburger with fries and salad	2 slices of roast lamb, ½ cup potatoes & broccoli
10 PM	1 cup yogurt with a snack or cookie	1 muffin	1 slice of cake	1 medium apple	1 orange	popcorn	1 cookie

This may look somewhat overwhelming to you right now but remember this is your pathway to freedom. First, eat what you can without bingeing and purging, taking laxatives or over-exercising, and slowly building up from there.

"Any weight you may or may not gain will fall off naturally as your body balances out and your powerful metabolism speeds up."

STRUCTURED EATING PROGRAM PLAN

Complete this table to plan your meals for the week. Then, each week, become more organized with your plans of your weekly meals. At the end of the Workbook is a link to a downloadable PDF to print out and complete weekly.

TABLE 13: STRUCTURED EATING PROGRAM PLAN

TIME	MEAL AND SNACKS	MONDAY	TUESDAY	WEDNESDAY	THURSDAY	FRIDAY	SATURDAY	SUNDAY
7.30 AM	BREAKFAST							
11 AM	SNACK							
1 PM	LUNCH							
4 PM	SNACK							
7 PM	DINNER							
10 PM	SNACK							

BOOM!

STRUCTURED EATING PROGRAM WEEKLY DIARY

Complete this structured eating program weekly diary. Complete what foods you've eaten that week and look back over the weeks to see how you're progressing. Each week, ask yourself what you can introduce into your structured eating program for the following week and build from there. At the end of the Workbook is a link to a downloadable PDF to print out and complete weekly.

TABLE 14: STRUCTURED EATING PROGRAM WEEKLY DIARY

TIME	MEAL AND SNACKS	MONDAY	TUESDAY	WEDNESDAY	THURSDAY	FRIDAY	SATURDAY	SUNDAY
7.30 AM	BREAKFAST							
11 AM	SNACK							
1 PM	LUNCH							
4 PM	SNACK							
7 PM	DINNER							
10 PM	SNACK							

BOOM!

'REDUCE THE BEASTLY ABUSE' CONNECTED TO YOUR STRUCTURED MEAL PROGRAM

Let's break down these beastly rantings and complicated feelings about beginning your structured meal program. Fill out this table and then list which techniques you can start using to change your thinking and feeling.

EXERCISE: 'REDUCE THE BEASTLY ABUSE' CONNECTED TO YOUR STRUCTURED MEAL PROGRAM

DATE/TIME	WHAT HAPPENED THAT CAUSED YOU TO THINK & FEEL THIS WAY?	YOUR THOUGHTS & FEELINGS CONNECTED TO USING YOUR STRUCTURED MEAL PROGRAM	TECHNIQUES TO USE TO CHANGE YOUR THINKING & FEELING
Example	I ate one whole slice of toast	"I'm going to get fat now and feel dreadful"	"Spin and Win" technique
1.			
2.			
3.			
4.			
5.			
6.			
7.			
8.			
9.			
10.			

TECHNIQUES FOR HOW TO REDUCE THE BEASTLY ABUSE

Once you've learned each technique, return to this table and complete this checklist of techniques for you to consider using to work with and reduce fearful, distressing thoughts and feelings connected to this massive change with your structured meal program.

TABLE 15: TECHNIQUES FOR HOW TO REDUCE THE BEASTLY ABUSE

TECHNIQUE	MONDAY ✓	TUESDAY ✓	WEDNESDAY ✓	THURSDAY ✓	FRIDAY ✓	SATURDAY ✓	SUNDAY ✓
1. STEP INTO "A NEW YOU"							
2. "SHRINK & BLINK"							
3. "INSTANT TRIGGER CHANGE"							
4. "ELECTRIFY YOUR MOTIVATION"							
5. "URGE SURFING"							
6. "THOUGHT STOPPING"							
7. "SPIN & WIN"							
8. "SHATTER THAT HABIT"							
9. "EFT" TAP TAP TAP							
10. "INSPIRE YOUR SMOLDERING FIRE"							
11. "MOTIVATION BOOSTER"							

"When you starve yourself, you're only feeding your leprechaun"

THE FEARFUL FOODS

Do you have forbidden foods that you think may cause you to binge and purge, abuse laxatives/diuretics, or overexercise? Bad foods that you qualify as your trigger foods?

If this is the case, when you feel ready, expose yourself to these foods and the anxiety will begin to lessen. You'll feel less afraid, less fearful of these foods.

So, I would like you to make a list of all your bad/fearful foods, starting with the least challenging up to the most challenging. Work through the list over time, eating each fearful food at least five times. If it still makes you fearful, then take your time, and when you're ready and feel calmer, eat it again.

Do this as many times as you need to. Then, move on to the next fearful food on your list until you've worked through them all. Once completed, start to introduce them to your eating program.

TABLE 16: THE FEARFUL FOODS

SCALE 1 – 10 (10 = MOST FEARFUL)	FOOD Briefly describe the actual food	LEPRECHAUNS THOUGHTS Write the automatic thoughts that accompany the feelings before	WHAT YOUR HEALTHY POSITIVE VOICE IS TELLING YOU
		"Don't eat it; it will tip you over the edge." "I'm too scared if I eat this, I'll get fat"	You CAN eat this food. You'll be fine. It's okay to feel scared

As you do this, give yourself positive motivational phrases of encouragement.

For example: "I'm learning to eat this food, and as I do so, I feel calm and relaxed."

"Whenever you find yourself doubting how far you can go, just remember how far you have come" UNKNOWN

STEP 5

How Can I Get out of This Dark Hole?

"Shouting stop at that negative self-talk allows
the calmness inside to…. Breathe"
KATE HUDSON-HALL

TABLE 17: YOUR OLD/NEW LIMITING BELIEFS EXAMPLE
TABLE 18: YOUR OLD/NEW LIMITING BELIEFS
TABLE 19: CHANGE YOUR BELIEFS INSTANTLY TECHNIQUE
TABLE 20: STRESSOMETER & SCALE
EXERCISE: CALM THAT ALARM

HOW CAN I GET OUT OF THIS DARK HOLE?

Climb out of your dark hole by working through the different exercises and tables and adjoining techniques to begin to break through your negative behaviors and take small steps up your ladder.

As you begin to change, you'll feel empowered to continue step by step.

BELIEFS

What's a belief?

A belief is the confidence you have about what something means. Your beliefs create maps that guide you toward the good or bad you have in your life. They come from past experiences, whether they were a painful or enjoyable experience.

What's a limiting belief?

Your limiting belief is something you believe to be true about yourself, someone else, or the world that limits you somehow. These beliefs hold you back from moving forward, keeping you stuck, focusing on the negative aspects of your behavior.

It's time to replace your old, disempowering beliefs with new empowering beliefs, but first, you need to identify what your old beliefs are.

Key elements for your new belief:

- It has to be simple and specific
- It has to address the old belief
- It has to be opened and revisable

YOUR OLD/NEW BELIEFS EXAMPLE

Looking through the example list of old and new beliefs, identify your old beliefs. Then hop to "Your Old/New Beliefs Table" and begin to list your old limiting beliefs. Then it's time to create new beliefs to focus on instead.

TABLE 17: OLD/NEW BELIEFS EXAMPLE

OLD BELIEF	NEW BELIEF
"People who are thin are pretty"	"I can be happy however I look." "I am worthy of living my life free from bulimia"
"I must be perfect and not make mistakes"	"It is okay to make some mistakes"
"I'm not good enough"	"I am good enough to live a free and happy life"
"I'm worthless "I'm not worthy of living without bulimia"	"Each day, I am learning to love myself more"
"I have no control over my eating"	"I am learning to be in total control of the foods I eat"
"If I'm fat, I'll be unlovable"	"I am taking steps to believe I am loveable"

YOUR OLD/NEW BELIEFS

Looking through the example list, make a list of all your limiting beliefs. Once you've identified your old beliefs, then look again through the list of new beliefs in the example list and begin to create new super powerful beliefs to focus on instead.

TABLE 18: YOUR OLD/NEW LIMITING BELIEFS

YOUR OLD BELIEF	YOUR NEW BELIEF
1.	
2.	
3.	
4.	
5.	
6.	
7.	
8.	
9.	
10.	

BOOM!

"CHANGE YOUR BELIEFS INSTANTLY" TECHNIQUE

Use this table in conjunction with the "Change your beliefs instantly" technique to help you modify your old limiting belief and create a new empowering belief using the submodalities from the belief you know is true, your certain belief.

Otherwise, pop to the end of the book and download the "Change your beliefs instantly" technique and watch the video demonstration.

TABLE 19: "CHANGE YOUR BELIEFS INSTANTLY" TECHNIQUE

SUBMODALITES	LIMITING BELIEF	CERTAIN BELIEF (Something you know is true)	NEW EMPOWERING BELIEF
WHAT IMAGES DO YOU HAVE?			
WHAT ARE YOU SAYING TO YOURSELF			
WHAT ARE YOU FEELING?			
IS IT CLOSE UP OR FAR AWAY?			
COLOR OR BLACK AND WHITE			
MOVING OR STILL			
ARE YOU LOOKING AT THE PICTURE OR IN THE PICTURE?			

BOOM!

STRESSOMETER

How stressed are you right now?

We can't avoid stressful experiences. They're always lurking around one corner or another. Your goal is to begin to manage your stress skilfully. A crucial part of this is to be aware of your internal worry and your devious leprechaun and his thoughts and stories, as they contribute to your stress. Your stress levels are directly related to your interpretation of an event that triggers the stress.

Each day, I would like you to rate where you are on the stressometer scale. Write this in the table and then start to use your new relaxation breathing technique and create a new habit to begin to calm you when you're feeling stressed.

Keeping tabs on your stress levels and what causes you to zip up that scale will remind you to practice your breathing technique to reduce that stress and create a positive new habit instantly.

STRESSOMETER SCALE

With the stressometer scale, the rate where you are from 0 to 10, how stressed, anxious, scared, or tense do you feel?

STRESSOMETER SCALE

TABLE 20: STRESSOMETER

List a stressful event and rate where you are on the scale from 0 – 10

THE STRESSFUL EVENT	MONDAY SCALE 0 - 10	TUESDAY SCALE 0 - 10	WEDNESDAY SCALE 0 - 10	THURSDAY SCALE 0 - 10	FRIDAY SCALE 0 - 10	SATURDAY SCALE 0 - 10	SUNDAY SCALE 0 - 10

EXERCISE: CALM THAT ALARM

Once you have your list of stressful events and your rating on your scale, when you're feeling stressed, upset, anxious, or scared and need a fantastic way to calm yourself, do the following:

LEARN HOW TO RESPOND RATHER THAN REACT

A.   With the stressometer scale, rate where you would be from 0 – 10, how stressed, anxious, scared, or tense do you feel?

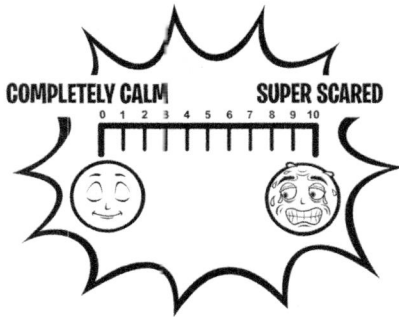

Rate on the STRESSOMETER SCALE AND BREATH, NOT SEETHE...

B.   Then take one big deep breath, breathing in through your nose for the count of four down into your stomach. Then breathe out through your mouth to the count of eight. When you breathe out, purse your lips and gently blow like you're blowing out a candle or bubble.

Repeat B as many times as your rating on the stressometer. If you rate 10, repeat this 10 times. Keep a log of how often you're practicing this to create a new positive habit and then keep rating throughout the week. So, whenever you feel stressed, you'll use your breathing technique. It works! It's an excellent super-fast way to clear your fuzzy mind and calm that alarm immediately.

STEP 6

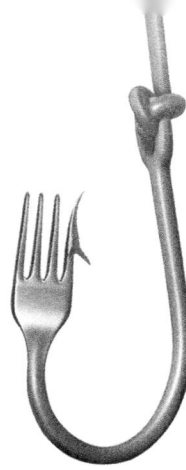

I Dont Want to Put on Weight, Will This Happen?

"By changing nothing, nothing changes" TONY ROBBINS

EXERCISE: HOW DO YOU FEEL ABOUT YOUR BODY IMAGE
BODY IMAGE AFFIRMATIONS & EXERCISE
TABLE 21: AFFIRMATION EXAMPLES AND NEW AFFIRMATIONS
EXERCISE: WEIGH NOT, WANT NOT
TABLE 22: HOW TO BEAT YOUR BLOATING BEAST

I DONT WANT TO PUT ON WEIGHT, WILL THIS HAPPEN?

As you follow your eating program, you may or MAY NOT put weight on, but it could impact your weight. Of course, everyone is different, and you may stay the same weight or put on a small amount of weight.

But once you've followed your eating program, and as long as you eat intuitively and exercise, your weight will eventually stabilize!

Think about all that you've put your body through with Bulimia: living on empty, with no fuel, severely dehydrated, plus all the other struggles it has had.

When you start to eat fantastic nutritious food again, your metabolism will speed up, rehydrate you, and give you newfound energy over time.

As you take that first step in your eating program and the first morsel passes through your body, every single cell starts to celebrate and goes from a shriveled raisin into a flourishing rehydrated beefy grape.

EXERCISE: HOW DO YOU FEEL ABOUT YOUR BODY IMAGE?

LET'S LEARN ABOUT HOW YOU FEEL, WHAT YOU THINK AND SEE WITH REGARDS TO YOUR BODY IMAGE

You must have a clearer understanding of how you feel and think about your body image to begin to change what you're doing, as it's not working right now. To help you tune into what you're really thinking and feeling, complete these questions:

How do you feel about your body?

_____

_____

_____

What are your thoughts about your body? What do you:

Like?

_____

_____

_____

Dislike?

_____

_____

_____

Think back to when you first started not to like your body. What else was happening in your life?

_____

_____

_____

Why is it so important to have the perfect body?

_____

_____

_____

What could you change now to begin to build on a healthier relationship with your body? For example:

Begin to change your habit of weighing yourself regularly

Begin to change how often you check yourself in the mirror

Begin to change how often you ask others for reassurance

Begin to change how often you check the size of your body with a tape measure

_____

_____

_____

Writing down how you can start to create a healthier relationship with your body is a significant positive step forward. Use the techniques in *Bulimia Sucks!* to help you with any distressing thoughts, feelings, or images you may have about your body and the changes you're making.

BODY IMAGE AFFIRMATIONS

What could help you begin to change how you feel about your body is working with the techniques from *Bulimia Sucks!* listed at the back of this book with the video demonstration links. These will help you to learn how to overpower your negative thoughts and feelings. Another great way is with affirmations.

We all have our days when we don't feel too comfortable in our bodies. You can move forward with this and start to learn how to develop a positive body image and recognize and respect your natural body image and shape by giving yourself accepting, positive affirmations daily. Oh yes, but what's an affirmation?

An affirmation is a short, simple, positive phrase that you repeat to yourself throughout the day to redirect your thinking and speaking into positive thought patterns.

It should be a phrase that instantly creates a compelling picture of yourself, looking and feeling the way you want to be. Again, this is working with our unconscious mind to guide it toward helping you move forward in your life, clearly telling it you're taking responsibility to change.

It's having a conscious, specific phrase that will help create something new or help reduce something from your life.

For affirmations to work, one requirement is that they must be believable and another is that they must not contain negative words such as "not." Otherwise, the unconscious mind won't see the "not" and focus on the next word.

It's time to check out the affirmation examples in the affirmation table. Which ones resonate with you? Then create your own realistic and suitable affirmations.

TABLE 21: AFFIRMATION EXAMPLES AND NEW AFFIRMATIONS

AFFIRMATION EXAMPLES	YOUR NEW AFFIRMATION
"My body deserves my kindness"	
"My body needs me to provide it with healthy foods so that I can live a happy life"	
"I thank my body for its strength and resilience"	
"I respect my body with loving thoughts and healthy choices"	
"I deserve love from myself and others"	
"I care for my body by caring for myself"	
"I am okay, just the way I am"	
"I appreciate my body, and I'm going to give it the nourishment that it needs from me"	
"I will be kind to myself for making mistakes or feeling down"	
"It's okay for me to love myself!"	

When you repeat your affirmation, create an image in your mind of yourself being this way. Make the image big, bright, bold, and colorful. Feel what it's like to have what you want. Make this image into a movie, and you're the star, enjoying feeling good.

Practice this daily, repeating the affirmation as many times as possible, eventually building up to over 100 times a day. Take the movie you've made with you wherever you go. Repetition is the key.

Write your affirmation on a post-it note and pop it up around your house to remind you to repeat it.

Anthony Robbins says:

"By repeating an affirmation over and over again, it becomes embedded in the subconscious mind, and eventually becomes your reality. That is why you need to be careful what you think and believe because that is exactly what you get!"

EXERCISE: WEIGH NOT, WANT NOT

Weight gain can be such a massive hindrance in recovery. The more you can identify your issues around putting on weight, the easier it will be to work with these and loosen their grip and the less difficult your recovery will be.

What if you do put on some weight? What does that mean to you?

- For some, being fat means being less popular, less in control, unhappy, not good enough, sad
- For some being thin means being popular, in control, happy, and confident

Ask yourself these questions:

What does being thin mean to you?

_____

_____

_____

What does being fat mean to you?

_____

_____

_____

Look at the link between the two. What does this mean to you and is it actually true?

_____

_____

_____

Having a clearer understanding of precisely what you're worried about if you do put weight on, which is usually only temporary, is what you've written in your answers really reliant on how you look with your weight?

Probably NOT, people will like or love you no matter what weight you are!

HOW TO BEAT YOUR BLOATING BEAST

Bonus Exercise It can take time for your body to change from the survival mode to a positive, healthy working body. So, a little weight could well be put on. But let me reassure you; this is okay. It's a common symptom of recovery, probably due to bloating, sometimes referred to as the "bulimia bloat" or "recovery bloat," which is a frequent pattern in recovery as your body begins to adjust and balance out.

Remember: **Your bloating is NOT real weight gain.**
It's NOT you getting fat.
It's the bulimia bloat and is TEMPORARY.
Your stomach will REDUCE.

Think About This Now...

This is a list of what you can physically begin to change to ward off the problematic thoughts and feelings connected to the bloating beast.

Complete the bloating beast table and then add your own ideas of what you can do differently.

TABLE 22: HOW TO BEAT YOUR BLOATING BEAST

CHANGES TO MAKE	DONE ✓	TO DO & KEEP DOING!
GRADUALLY BUILD ON YOUR WATER INTAKE		
SIDE STEP ALCOHOL AND CAFFEINE, as these liquids, lead to water retention		
TAKE GENTLE EXERCISE		
AVOID THOSE MIRRORS!		
SLOW YOUR EATING DOWN		
SPEAK TO YOUR DOCTOR RE: SUPPLEMENTS		
TOSS THOSE SCALES!		
WEAR LOOSE CLOTHING		
SPEND TIME WITH SUPPORTIVE PEOPLE		
TAP TAP TAP on all of your distress of putting on weight		
CREATE A NEW POSITIVE AFFIRMATION		
LIST 3 OTHER CHANGES YOU CAN MAKE TO BEAT YOUR BULIMIA BLOAT: 1. 2. 3.		

To beat this bloating beast, you have to keep eating, keep nourishing your body with adequate nutrients and sufficient calories consistently.

"The greatest weapon against stress is the ability to choose one thought over another" WILLIAM JAMES

STEP 7

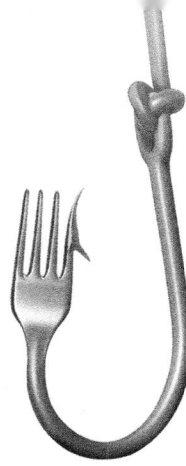

How Can I Change All My Negative Habits?

"Motivation may be what starts you off, but it's habit that keeps you going back for more" MIYA YAMANOUCHI

HOW CAN I CHANGE ALL MY NEGATIVE HABITS?

Oh yes, this is a great question. Well, one way to begin to change negative habits is first to become aware of what your unhealthy habits are and then learn how to create new positive habits. So, read on…

WHAT IS A HABIT?

Habits are sequences of actions that we carry out routinely on autopilot to make our lives easier, acting as shortcuts that allow us to use our energy on more critical areas of our lives. Of course, over time, we've created good positive habits. But, alas, we've also created the not so good habits.

Having Bulimia isn't your fault! It's the natural result of your mental programming at this moment in time.

How do I create new habits?

Creating a new positive habit can be so powerful and lead you to beneficial and encouraging life changes. We're all creatures of habit. We're relying on our past learned behaviors and habits to make our decisions.

As you create a habit, your brain has developed neuro-pathways that unfold as your automatic go-to habits.

It takes conscious action and practice to form your habit. Therefore, it takes intentional action and training to break your habit. Or better still, replace it with an excellent positive habit.

Let's begin to understand your habit cycle. You can't change a habit without understanding how they work individually for you. What precisely are the steps?

There are three steps to the process:

- A trigger
- A routine
- A reward

Earlier in the Workbook, you began to identify the specific triggers and rewards of your Bulimia. For example, the reasons why you make yourself sick.

Hop back to Step 1, and read through the identified function, rewards, or needs of your behavior. For example, "It's my way to distract me from the stress of daily life."

So, you engage in your habit of bingeing and purging to gain some sort of rewards like numbing your emotions, relieving boredom, or time for you.

Examples of rewards:

- Weight loss
- Release of dopamine
- Relief from overeating
- Comfort
- Detachment from feelings

If there's repetition, the habit develops.

As you become aware of your habit behavior that fires up your urges, you can begin to break the habit pattern. A habit diary will help you achieve this.

HABIT DIARY

Complete the HABIT DIARY table to help you identify your habit behaviors that sweep you into your urges, and then you can start to break this habit pattern.

TABLE 23: HABIT DIARY

DATE/ TIME	YOUR HABIT	WHERE ARE YOU? WHO ARE YOU WITH?	WHAT WERE YOU DOING JUST BEFORE THE HABIT?	THOUGHTS AND FEELINGS AND IMAGES JUST BEFORE THE HABIT?	THOUGHTS AND FEELINGS AND IMAGES DURING THE HABIT?	THOUGHTS AND FEELINGS AND IMAGES AFTER THE HABIT?	YOUR REWARD/ PLEASURE?
Example	Jumping onto the scales	At home, on own	Getting dressed, jeans feel tighter	"I'm fatter." Image of bulges over tops of jeans. Feel angry	Panic, scared, worthless	"I must not eat anything today." Feel sad, lonely, a failure	Bingeing and purging
1.							
2.							
3.							
4.							
5.							
6.							
7.							
8.							
9.							
10.							

BOOM!

CREATE A NEW POSITIVE HABIT

Now you have your list of habits that drive you to binge and purge. This table is to work in conjunction with the "Shatter that Habit" technique. Otherwise, zip to the end of the book and download the "Shatter that Habit" technique steps and watch the video demonstration.

Learning the "Shatter that Habit" technique will help you stay motivated and permanently change your habit. You'll be stepping out of the old you and then seeing yourself how you would like to be in the future, making that image so powerful that it draws you into being the kind of person who is free from that old harmful habit.

Complete this table to assist you in having a clear understanding of the old habits you've identified and then creating new positive habits to guide you in stepping toward your freedom from Bulimia.

TABLE 24: CREATE A NEW POSITIVE HABIT

OLD HABIT IDENTIFIED	NEW POSITIVE HABIT
Example "I want to stop stressing about everything"	"Every time I have a stressed feeling, I am going to take 3 deep breaths and relax"
1.	1.
2.	2.
3.	3.
4.	4.
5.	5.
6.	6.
7.	7.
8.	8.
9.	9.
10.	10.

BOOM!

LAXATIVE CAUSES & NEW COPING STRATEGIES

So, what's causing you to reach out for the laxatives? Yes, your thoughts and feelings, so complete the table of what's causing you to reach out for the laxatives, listing your thoughts and feelings.

Then to challenge these, create new powerful positive coping strategies.

TABLE 25: LAXATIVE CAUSES & NEW COPING STRATEGIES

THE CAUSES:	NEW COPING STRATEGIES:
1.	1.
2.	2.
3.	3.
4.	4.
5.	5.
6.	6.
7.	7.
8.	8.
9.	9.
10.	10.

DIURETICS CAUSES & NEW COPING STRATEGIES

So, what's causing you to reach out for the diuretics? Yes, your thoughts and feelings, so complete the table of what's causing you to reach out for the diuretics, listing your thoughts and feelings. Then to challenge these, create new powerful positive coping strategies.

TABLE 26: DIURETICS CAUSES & NEW COPING STRATEGIES

THE CAUSES:	NEW COPING STRATEGIES:
1.	1.
2.	2.
3.	3.
4.	4.
5.	5.
6.	6.
7.	7.
8.	8.
9.	9.
10.	10.

OVEREXERCISING CAUSES & NEW COPING STRATEGIES

So, what's causing you to overexercise? Yes, your thoughts and feelings, so complete the table of what's causing you to reach out for the exercise equipment, listing your thoughts and feelings. Then to challenge these, create new powerful positive coping strategies.

TABLE 27: OVEREXERCISING CAUSES & NEW COPING STRATEGIES

THE CAUSES:	NEW COPING STRATEGIES:
1.	1.
2.	2.
3.	3.
4.	4.
5.	5.
6.	6.
7.	7.
8.	8.
9.	9.
10.	10.

"You can't start the next chapter of your life if you keep rereading the last one" MICHAEL MCMILLIAN

STEP 8

Are You Scared about the Changes? This Step Is All about Tapping!

"The secret of change is to focus all your energy, not on fighting the old, but on building the new." SOCRATES

EMOTIONAL FREEDOM TECHNIQUE (EFT for short or the tapping technique.)
TABLE 28: I'M SCARED THOUGHTS AND FEELINGS
TABLE 29: I'M SCARED OF LIVING WITHOUT BULIMIA
TABLE 30: I'M SCARED OF LIVING WITH BULIMIA
TABLE 31: I'M SCARED OF LOSING CONTROL
TABLE 32: I'M SCARED OF WHO I AM WITHOUT BULIMIA
TABLE 33: I'M SCARED OF PUTTING ON WEIGHT
TABLE 34: I'M SCARED THAT THE WEIGHT GAIN WILL BE TOO FAST
TABLE 35: I'M SCARED IF I DO START EATING, I'LL NEVER STOP

I'M SCARED ABOUT ALL THE CHANGES, SO WHAT IS TAPPING?

Yes, I get it, I was super scared about all the changes I had to make to begin changing my patterns. So, to help you address your multitude of scared feelings, negative thoughts, and worries, I'm going to teach you a specific technique called Emotional Freedom Technique (EFT for short or the tapping technique.)

EFT therapy is a simple yet very powerful way to overcome any painful feelings or emotions that stop you from beginning to break free from your old past urges and patterns. It's a fantastic tool to have in your pocket for any negative feelings at any time.

So many of my clients have hugely benefited from tapping whenever they have any negative feelings. They're amazed by how quickly this process can reduce these horrific feelings they may be having.

The excellent news about EFT is that:

- It's a quick therapy, and you won't need to relive painful memories
- Once you've learned the points, you can tap on any difficult feelings.
- You can take it with you wherever you go if you're feeling uneasy. You can just do a round of tapping to reduce the uncomfortable feeling
- It only takes minutes to dissolve negative feelings

HERE'S HOW YOU'RE GOING TO CHANGE NOW WITH EFT:

Using the fingertips of your index and middle finger of either hand, you tap approximately 5-7 times on each point.

Firmly but gently tap either side of the body as outlined below:

- KC: The Karate Chop point (abbreviated KC). This is located at the center of the fleshy part of the outside of your hand (either hand), between the top of the wrist and the base of the baby finger. Or the part of your hand you would use to deliver a karate chop
- EB: At the beginning of the eyebrow just above and to one side of the nose
- SE: On the bone bordering the outside corner of the eye, on the side of the eye
- UE: On the bone under an eye about 1 inch below your pupil. Under the eye
- UN: On the small area between the bottom of your nose and the top of your upper lip. Under the nose
- CH: Midway between the point of your chin and the bottom of your lower lip. Even though it's not directly on the point of the chin, we call it the chin point because it's descriptive enough for people to understand easily
- CB: The junction where the sternum (breastbone), collarbone, and the first rib meet
- UA: On the side of the body, at a point even with the nipple (for men) or in the middle of the bra strap (for women). It's about 4 inches below the armpit
- TOH: On the top of the head. If you were to draw a line from one ear, over the head, to the other ear, and another line from your nose to the back of your neck, the TOH point is where those two lines would intersect.

THE 5 STEPS OF THE EFT TAPPING BASIC RECIPE

1. Identify the specific feeling that you're going to tap on. (Only focus on one particular negativity at a time). Examples might be, feeling scared, hopeless, worthless, guilty, or shameful, although you could tap on any negative feeling you're having.

2. Test the initial intensity: I want you to think of a scale between 0–10, with 0 being the feeling has gone entirely and 10 being at its most intense. This gives you a guide, as you'll review your scale after each round of tapping to compare the progress.

   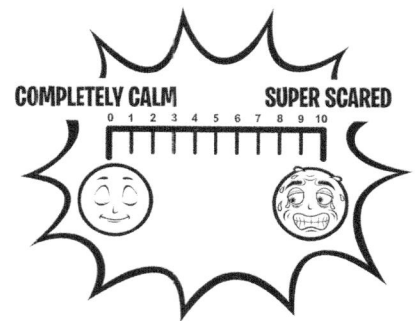

   COMPLETELY CALM   SUPER SCARED
   0 1 2 3 4 5 6 7 8 9 10

   If you're tapping on a feeling, you can recreate the memories in your imagination to make it easier to gauge where you would be on the scale.

   If you're tapping on physical pain, tune into the pain, and assess the level.

3. The next step is to repeat a simple phrase while tapping continuously on your karate chop point (KC). You would do this by saying:

"Even though I have this_____, I deeply and completely accept myself."

Fill in the blank for whatever specific emotion you're working on.

For example:

*   Even though I feel embarrassed and disgusted with myself, I deeply and completely accept myself
*   Even though these urges are so overwhelming, I deeply and completely accept myself
*   Even though I have failed, I deeply and completely accept myself
*   Even though bingeing and purging is my secret, and I'm so disgusted with myself, I deeply and completely accept myself
*   Even though I feel I have no control over my bingeing and purging, I deeply and completely accept myself
*   Even though I'm scared of anyone finding out because they would reject me, I deeply and completely accept myself

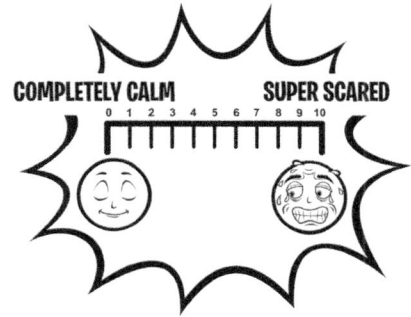

4. Next, we're going to move on to tapping on each of the points listed while saying a reminder phrase. So rather than saying the whole long phrase as you've just done tapping on your karate chop point. You're going to reduce it to one or two words. For example, "these urges," "failure," "no control," "I'm scared," anything that's going to help you to stay tuned in to your issue.

Here's the list of the points below:

Beginning of the Eyebrow (EB)
Side of the Eye (SE)
Under the Eye (UE)
Under the Nose (UN)
Chin Point (CH)
Beginning of the Collarbone (CB)
Under the Arm (UA)
Top of the Head (TOH)

5. Now go back to your scale and see where you are and how the issue has reduced in intensity.

If you aren't down to zero, then repeat the process until you either achieve zero or plateau at some level.

EFT (EMOTIONAL FREEDOM TECHNIQUE) TAPPING POINTS

#8 - TOH
#1 - EB
#2 - SE
#3 - UE
#4 - UN
#5 - CH
#6 - CB
#7 - UA

Karate chop point

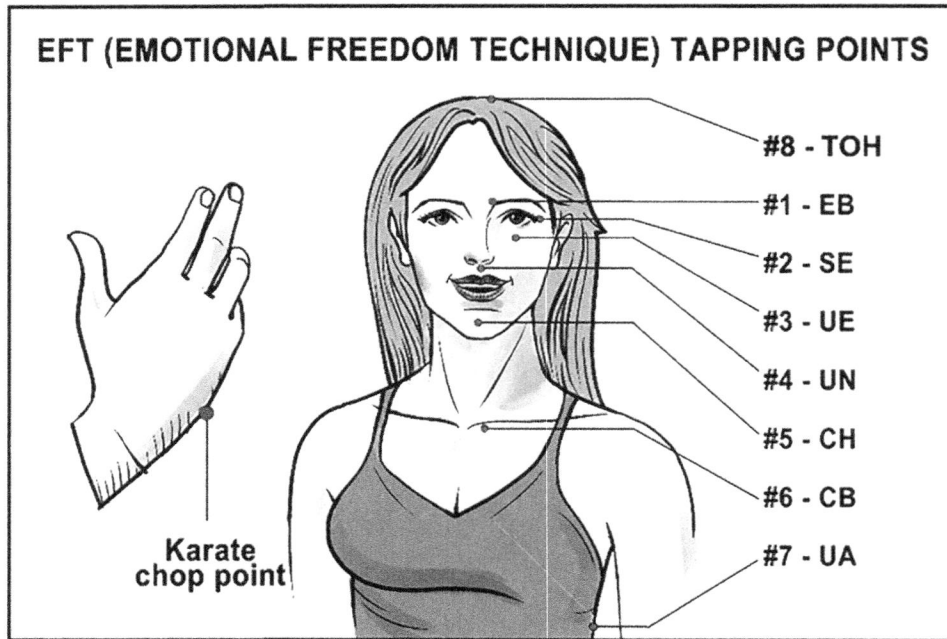

Fantastic, this is so simple to learn, and once you've learned the points and how this process works, it's an incredible way to reduce those negative thoughts and feelings, as you can tap on whatever feelings you have. But be as specific as possible when focusing on your feelings.

I've found EFT to be extremely useful in treating the many issues connected to Bulimia and other eating disorders. Anger problems, anxiety disorders, and stress in particular, especially where clients have tried other treatments that haven't been successful (Craig & Craig, n.d.).

To see a video demonstration of EFT, zip to the end of the book for the link.

BOOM!

I'M SCARED THOUGHTS AND FEELINGS

So, when you start to take the decisive positive steps toward moving forward in your life:

How do you feel? How scared are you to begin? What's stopping you?

Tune in to all your thoughts and feelings and complete your thoughts and feelings table with any complicated, painful feelings and thoughts that may come up.

I call it a "scared feeling throughout this step," but for you, it might be a different feeling. So, tune into your frequency and see what comes up.

Please fill out the table including your scale before, then tap on it, adding your scale after. If it's not down to a 0, then keep tapping and then you'll end up like a finely tuned piano!

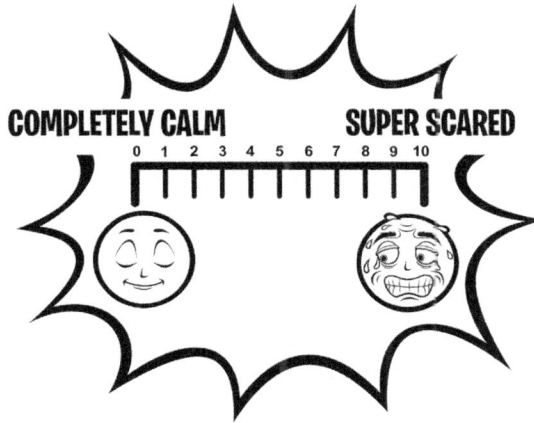

COMPLETELY CALM   **SUPER SCARED**

0 1 2 3 4 5 6 7 8 9 10

TABLE 28: I'M SCARED THOUGHTS AND FEELINGS

SCARED/PAINFUL/TERRIFYING THOUGHTS AND FEELINGS ABOUT CHANGING AND FREEING YOURSELF OF BULIMIA	SCALE BEFORE	SCALE AFTER
Example: "Even though I'm scared of all my feelings, I deeply accept myself"		
1.		
2.		
3.		
4.		
5.		
6.		
7.		
8.		
9.		
10.		

I'M SCARED OF LIVING WITHOUT BULIMIA

Does the thought of living life without bulimia terrify you?

For you, bulimia may have become your identity. It's part of your life. It drives your actions and behaviors, influencing all your thoughts.

Even though a part of you wants to be free from bulimia, another part is scared to live without it. You may have tried in the past with thoughts of stopping, but the fear and panic come rushing back.

Do you wonder who you would be without the number on the scale defining your worth?

Do you wonder what you would do if you weren't running miles every day?

Do you wonder what people will think of you if you're not striving to be perfect?

It's time to separate from all of your negative thinking and discover your true identity and self.

Tune in to all your thoughts and feelings connected to living life without bulimia and complete your thoughts and feelings table with any difficult, painful feelings and thoughts that may come up. Once you have your list and scale before tapping, add your scale after, and work through your list to reduce what thoughts and feelings come up until you have each one down to a 0.

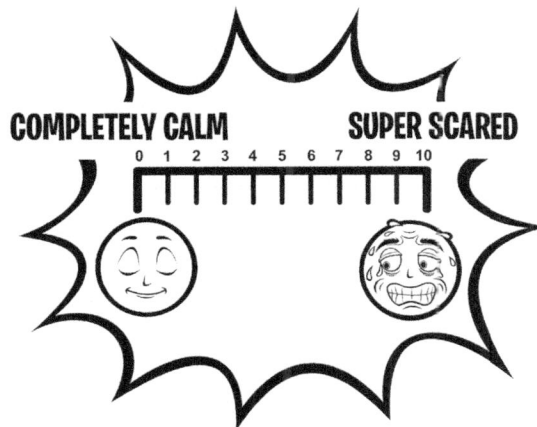

TABLE 29: I'M SCARED OF LIVING WITHOUT BULIMIA

THOUGHTS AND FEELINGS CONNECTED TO SCARED TO LIVE WITHOUT BULIMIA	SCALE BEFORE	SCALE AFTER
Example: "Even though bingeing and purging are my only way to cope with life, I deeply accept myself"		
1.		
2.		
3.		
4.		
5.		
6.		
7.		
8.		
9.		
10.		

I'M SCARED OF LIVING WITH BULIMIA

Yes, you absolutely may be scared of continuing to live with all these harmful habits and patterns of bingeing and purging and wishing you were someone else, knowing how it's damaging your body and your whole life.

But this doesn't mean you have to continue this way. It's your choice if you carry on thinking and behaving this way or start to change small patterns of thinking. And if you did, what would you change first?

Tune in to all your thoughts and feelings connected to precisely you're scared of living with bulimia and complete your thoughts and feelings table with any difficult, painful feelings and thoughts that may come up. Once you have your list and scale before tapping, add your scale after, and work through your list to reduce what thoughts and feelings come up until you have each one down to a 0.

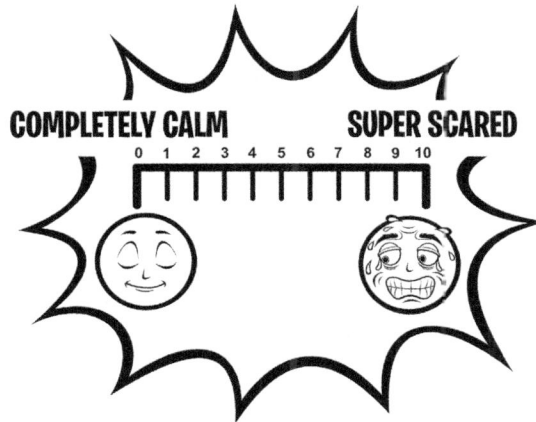

COMPLETELY CALM   **SUPER SCARED**

0 1 2 3 4 5 6 7 8 9 10

TABLE 30: I'M SCARED OF LIVING WITH BULIMIA

THOUGHTS AND FEELINGS CONNECTED TO SCARED TO LIVE WITHOUT BULIMIA	SCALE BEFORE	SCALE AFTER
Example: "Even though I know I'm damaging my body but can't stop, I deeply accept myself"		
1.		
2.		
3.		
4.		
5.		
6.		
7.		
8.		
9.		
10.		

I'M SCARED OF LOSING CONTROL

There may be many thoughts and feelings that come with losing control when you take that first step to recovery. But you do know how to be in control of yourself. You've done it before the bulimia and all the negative patterns started. It's there inside you, holding on, waiting for you to make that decision.

Recovery is all about change. Sometimes, the change may not be very comfortable. But as you're focusing on how you want to be in the future, the greater the reward will be.

Rather than view it as starting over, view it as a blank learning slate to slowly build on beginning to feel better about yourself. Learn to be curious rather than judgmental and critical of yourself. Begin to uncover patterns in your feelings and behaviors so you can learn to change them and be healthier and happier.

Tune in to all your thoughts and feelings connected to how scared you are of losing control and complete your thoughts and feelings table with any difficult, painful feelings and thoughts that may come up. Once you have your list and scale before tapping, add your scale after and work through your list to reduce what thoughts and feelings come up until you have each one down to a 0.

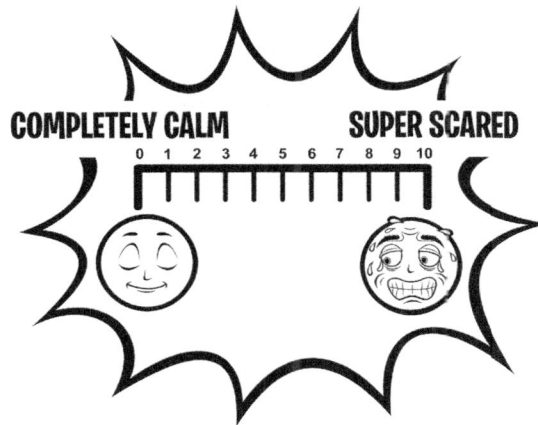

COMPLETELY CALM   SUPER SCARED
0 1 2 3 4 5 6 7 8 9 10

TABLE 31: I'M SCARED OF LOSING CONTROL

THOUGHTS AND FEELINGS CONNECTED TO SCARED TO LIVE WITHOUT BULIMIA	SCALE BEFORE	SCALE AFTER
Example: "Even though I'm scared I'll lose control without bulimia, I deeply accept myself"		
1.		
2.		
3.		
4.		
5.		
6.		
7.		
8.		
9.		
10.		

I'M SCARED OF WHO I AM WITHOUT BULIMIA

Ask yourself, "Who was I before the bulimia started?"

And you'll find that the first answer that comes into your head right now is the correct answer, directly from your unconscious mind.

As I mentioned in *Bulimia Sucks!* I'm reasonably sure you weren't a serial k_ller or something much worse. You were just YOU, without the negative learnings, patterns, and behaviors. Just fabulous YOU.

Tune in to all your thoughts and feelings connected to how scared of who you are without bulimia and complete your thoughts and feelings table with any difficult, painful feelings and thoughts that may come up. Once you have your list and scale, begin tapping, then add your scale after, work through your list, reducing what thoughts and feelings come up until you have each one down to a 0.

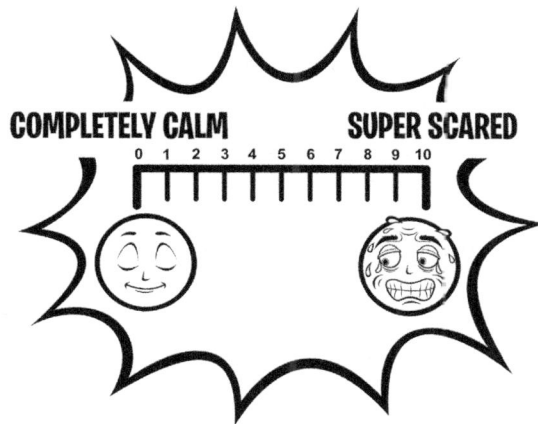

TABLE 32: I'M SCARED OF WHO I AM WITHOUT BULIMIA

THOUGHTS AND FEELINGS CONNECTED TO SCARED TO LIVE WITHOUT BULIMIA	SCALE BEFORE	SCALE AFTER
Example: "Even though I may not like myself without bulimia, I deeply accept myself"		
1.		
2.		
3.		
4.		
5.		
6.		
7.		
8.		
9.		
10.		

I'M SCARED OF PUTTING ON WEIGHT

Remember, if you do put on weight, it's only TEMPORARY. It won't last forever. Your weight will lessen.

It's your body adjusting to being fed and watered. You're just like a wilting flower. Provided food and water, you'll flourish into the blossoming beauty you were before the bulimia grabbed hold.

By now, you should be getting good at tapping and tuning in to what thoughts and feelings you're having,

Tune in to all your thoughts and feelings connected to how you feel about putting on weight and complete your thoughts and feelings table with any difficult, painful feelings and thoughts that may come up. Once you have your list and scale before tapping, add your scale after and work through your list to reduce what thoughts and feelings come up until you have each one down to a 0.

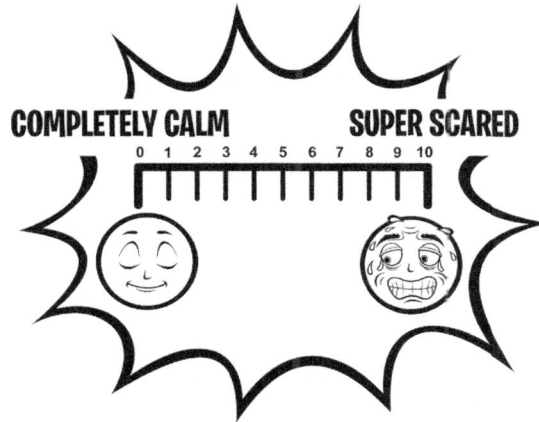

COMPLETELY CALM   **SUPER SCARED**

0 1 2 3 4 5 6 7 8 9 10

TABLE 33: I'M SCARED OF PUTTING ON WEIGHT

THOUGHTS AND FEELINGS CONNECTED TO SCARED TO LIVE WITHOUT BULIMIA	SCALE BEFORE	SCALE AFTER
Example: "Even though I'm scared to put weight on when I start on my structured eating program, I deeply accept myself"		
1.		
2.		
3.		
4.		
5.		
6.		
7.		
8.		
9.		
10.		

I'M SCARED THAT THE WEIGHT GAIN WILL BE TOO FAST?

Yes, this is a concern for all my clients in recovery but reread Step 6 again. If you do put weight on quickly, this will more likely be due to "the bulimia bloat" and will only be temporary. Your body isn't used to having food, so it may take time to adjust, but it will.

You can do this and deserve to live your life without bulimia.

Tune in to all your thoughts and feelings connected to how scared if the weight gain will be too fast. Complete your thoughts and feelings table with any difficult, painful feelings and thoughts that may come up. Once you have your list and scale before you begin tapping, then add your scale after, work through your list, reducing what thoughts and feelings come up until you have each one down to a 0.

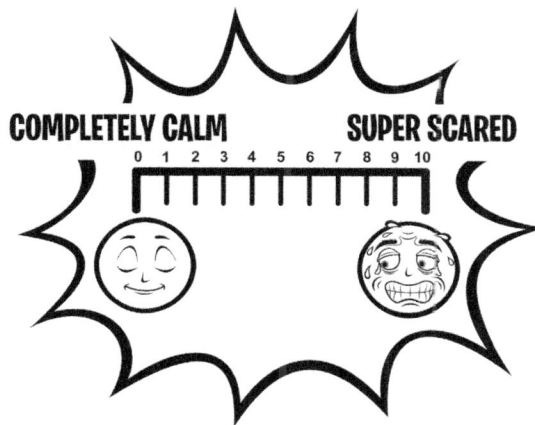

COMPLETELY CALM **SUPER SCARED**

0 1 2 3 4 5 6 7 8 9 10

TABLE 34: I'M SCARED THAT THE WEIGHT GAIN WILL BE TOO FAST?

THOUGHTS AND FEELINGS CONNECTED TO SCARED TO LIVE WITHOUT BULIMIA	SCALE BEFORE	SCALE AFTER
Example: "Even though I'm scared my weight gain will be too fast, I deeply accept myself"		
1.		
2.		
3.		
4.		
5.		
6.		
7.		
8.		
9.		
10.		

I'M SCARED IF I DO START EATING, I'LL NEVER STOP

I think you probably know the answer to this already. It will lead you to a binge. If that were to happen, that's okay. That's what recovery is all about: three or four steps forward and one step back to start with, or maybe not.

If this were to happen, don't beat yourself up. So be it! You can choose to let it go. Then figure out what you can learn from it. And, more importantly, what you can do differently next time.

Tune in to all your thoughts and feelings connected to how scared you are that when you start to eat, you'll never stop and complete your thoughts and feelings table with any difficult, painful feelings and thoughts that may come up. Once you have your list and scale before beginning tapping, add your scale after, work through your list, reduce what thoughts and feelings come up until you have each one down to a 0.

What specifically are you scared of if you don't stop eating?

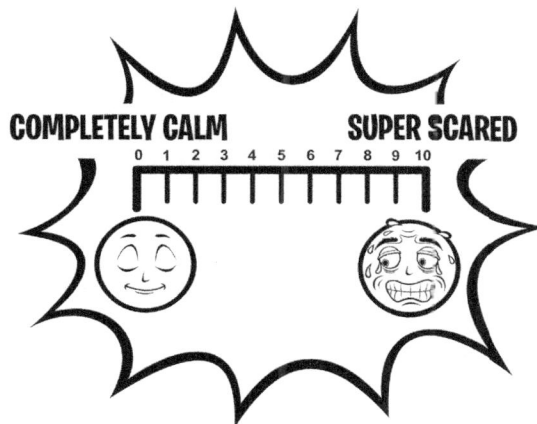

COMPLETELY CALM   SUPER SCARED
0 1 2 3 4 5 6 7 8 9 10

TABLE 35: I'M SCARED IF I DO START EATING, I'LL NEVER STOP

THOUGHTS AND FEELINGS CONNECTED TO SCARED TO LIVE WITHOUT BULIMIA	SCALE BEFORE	SCALE AFTER
Example: "Even though I might binge and purge and feel a failure if I can't stop eating, I deeply accept myself"		
1.		
2.		
3.		
4.		
5.		
6.		
7.		
8.		
9.		
10.		

BOOM!

"One reason people resist change is because they focus on what they have to give up instead of what they have to gain." RICK GODWIN

"The key to success is to focus on goals, not obstacles"

There are so many online groups you could join, so go check them out or come and join us on our Facebook page, https://www.facebook.com/groups/BulimiaSuck/

BOOM!

It can be reassuring or even inspiring to hear how others have dealt with different experiences with their bulimia and how they've moved forward in their recovery.

It's normal to have many difficult thoughts and feelings flapping within at the idea of telling someone about your bulimia. Nevertheless, my clients often say it wasn't so easy to tell their loved one, but the relief afterward was enormous, and the knowledge that the person is there to support them is a compelling motivator in their recovery.

_____

_____

_____

What can you do to help further yourself to feel more positive about reaching out for help?

For example: "It's not very helpful if you keep talking to me about what I've eaten. It would be more helpful if you were to ask me about how I'm feeling?" Whatever works for you.

Sometimes, people don't know the best things to say and can come out with something unhelpful. It's crucial that you speak up and give them a clear direction about what will help you.

_____

_____

_____

_____

Now make your own list of what they can do to begin to help you.

- Be patient
- Commenting on your strong points, interests, skills, and talents rather than how you look or your weight or shape
- Allow you to work through recovery at your own pace
- Be there to support you when you want to talk about how you feel
- Educate themselves on what bulimia is

For example:

3. How can they help YOU?

STEP 9

What Therapies Can Help Me?

"The battle within you today is giving you the strength you will feel tomorrow." KATE HUDSON-HALL

WHICH THERAPIES CAN HELP ME?
TABLE 36: MY SLIP UP WARNING SIGNS
EXERCISE: SLIP UP, HICCUP AND PICK YOURSELF UP PLAN
EXERCISE: YOUR PHYSICAL MAINTENANCE PLAN
EXERCISE: IS IT TIME TO REACH OUT FOR SUPPORT?

WHICH THERAPIES CAN HELP ME?

A wide variety of therapies can help you, but it's all about finding the right one that works for you.

Treatment for bulimia is most effective when it focuses, not so much on the eating behavior, although that's important, but on various areas like:

- Past events that could have triggered or influenced your relationship with food
- Depression, anger, and failure
- Reducing anxiety and stresses of life
- Exploring the connection between emotions and eating
- Addressing the idea that self-worth is based on weight

A multidirectional approach is often best when treating bulimia, anorexia, or any eating disorder.

SUGGESTIONS FOR THERAPIES THAT COULD HELP YOU:

Psychotherapy
Cognitive-Behavioral Therapy (CBT)
Hypnotherapy
Neuro Linguist Programming (NLP)
Mindfulness
Family Therapy
Nutrition Counseling
Group Therapy

For that support and guidance to freedom, research the many therapies and find the right one for you.

SLIP UPS

Research shows that how you talk to yourself about your slip-up can make a huge difference in your pathway toward recovery or slithering back down into your old behaviors.

For example: If you did slip up, you might say to yourself, "Well, I've done it again and failed, I'm hopeless, I knew I just couldn't change. Everyone will be so angry with me."

That will only make you feel terrible and, therefore, more than likely, continue slipping up.

But if you were to say, "Okay, I know, I'm so disappointed in myself when I felt so out of control. I know what I need to do differently if that happens again. Slip-ups happen, and that's okay, but I've made some good positive changes so far, and I can jump back on my horse and continue skipping along to freedom."

This is so much more positive and a skill that builds self–compassion. By building on becoming kinder to yourself, you'll learn to guide your way to a healthier relationship with yourself, which will help you stay focused easier on your goals to recovery.

The best way to deal with a slip-up is to understand that it's a possibility and may happen sometime. How would you manage this? Make a plan of action.

So, if you do slip up, remember, that's a natural path of recovery. Complete the TABLE: MY SLIP-UPS and start to learn from your slip-ups. The more you break down your slip-up pattern, the greater your understanding of what you can do differently to help you in your recovery.

TABLE 36: MY SLIP-UPS

WHAT ARE YOUR WARNING SIGNS?	YOUR THOUGHTS & FEELINGS	CHALLENGE THE THOUGHTS & FEELINGS
Making excuses for not eating	"My jeans are tighter" I feel panicked	I know not eating regularly is going to exacerbate the bulimia bloat
1.		
2.		
3.		
4.		
5.		
6.		
7.		
8.		
9.		
10.		

"People who wonder if the glass is half empty or half full miss the point. The glass is refillable." Unknown

SLIP UP, HICCUP AND PICK YOURSELF UP PLAN

Great, so now you have a better idea of your warning signs and your thoughts and feelings connected to your slip-up. Let's take this further and look at what caused the hiccup. What you could change if you were in the same situation, and what you need to do to refocus your mind and encourage you to hop back on your positive pathway.

EXERCISE: SLIP-UP, HICCUP, AND PICK YOURSELF UP PLAN

SLIP-UP BEHAVIOR	WHAT CAUSED THE HICCUP?	RETHINK WHAT YOU COULD CHANGE & DO DIFFERENTLY?	WHAT DO YOU NEED TO DO TO PICK YOURSELF UP GET BACK ON YOUR POSITIVE PATH?
Binged & purged. Took laxatives or diuretics, or overexercised	Not eating. "I was starving!"	Get organized with my meal plan & what foods I am going to eat	Continue eating regularly
1.			
2.			
3.			
4.			
5.			
6.			
7.			
8.			
9.			
10.			

EXERCISE: YOUR PHYSICAL MAINTENANCE PLAN

Imagine you had a car and you never took it for a service or any tests to check its oil, filter, brakes, tires, roadworthiness or tune it up to run at its peak condition. What would eventually happen to the car? It would give up the ghost, whatever that means, but it would eventually stop working.

Are you treating your body like a car?

More than likely. So, what you need to do is to begin looking at your self-care.

Keep regular tabs on what areas of self-care you may have overlooked ever since the leprechaun dug his heels in, such as visiting the doctor, therapist, dentist, physio, or nutritionist; updated your medications; smear/PAP tests; immunizations; birth control; joining support groups, or learning yoga or mindfulness.

Now is the time to start taking care of the whole of you…

Start by making a list of whom you need to make appointments with:

EXERCISE: YOUR PHYSICAL MAINTENANCE PLAN

TYPE OF MAINTENACE:	HOW OFTEN WEEKLY, MONTHLY OR YEARLY:	YOUR NEXT APPOINTMENT IS DUE:
For example, Therapist	Weekly	As soon as possible!
1.		
2.		
3.		
4.		
5.		
6.		
7.		
8.		
9.		
10.		

BOOM!

IS IT TIME TO REACH OUT FOR SUPPORT?

Are you ready to reach out for support now?

No? But when is the right time? 12th of…Never?

I would say NOW! But if you're not ready, let's break down your thoughts and feelings about telling your loved one. Because the better prepared you are, the more likely you are to step outside of your comfort zone and reach out for support.

SO, WHAT'S STOPPING YOU FROM REACHING OUT FOR SUPPORT?

It's time to be honest with yourself. Stop telling yourself that you're not that sick or that you have it under control. It's not working now and if no changes are made, it's not going to work anytime soon.

It's time to come clean with yourself; be truthful to that real you. Because you know, deep within, you're slipping down a terrifying path of ruining your health and negatively impacting your life and that of many other people.

Now is the time to address what's stopping you from reaching out for help and support. Let me tell you, it's not a sign of weakness but a sign of enormous courage and strength. It's not the first step into a court of judgment. It's your best opportunity for recovery and freedom from bulimia.

Many people out there desperately want to help and support you. You just need to find that inner strength to open up.

It's time to begin breaking down that big picture of what's stopping you specifically and working through these with the techniques in the *Bulimia Sucks!* book.

First, let's identify what stops you from even considering telling a friend or a loved one?

Complete these questions:

List the key areas that stop you from telling someone you have bulimia, including your thoughts, feelings, and reasons.

_____

_____

_____

_____

What can you do to begin to change these thoughts, feelings, and reasons?

You could:

- "EFT." Start tapping and work your way through everything on your list. Tap, tap, tap
- "SHRINK & BLINK" Use this to work with negative thoughts and images connected to that thought and blink it on and off until it disappeared
- "INSTANT TRIGGER CHANGE" technique. Just the thought of telling someone you have bulimia might be a trigger in itself and have you think about spiraling, so zip now to step 2 and work with the "INSTANT TRIGGER CHANGE" technique
- "CHANGE YOUR BELIEFS INSTANTLY" technique. Maybe a new belief has revealed itself to you regarding what's stopping you from recovery, or perhaps a big pile of them! So, zip back to step 6 and work with the "CHANGE YOUR BELIEFS INSTANTLY" technique
- "SPIN & WIN" technique. Another way to deal with your negative thoughts and feelings is with the "SPIN & WIN" technique from step 6. This is another fantastic tool to be able to change the way you feel quickly

Make your own list now of what you can do to change these thoughts, feelings, and reasons? Which techniques would you use?

_____

_____

_____

_____

_____

Whom to tell?

If you're not sure whom you would tell, think about all the people you know. Would it be a friend, loved one, therapist, teacher?

Think about whom you have confided in before? Or have you heard anyone discussing eating disorders or even any other mental health problems?

Create a list of possible supporters.

_____

_____

_____

When you tell your loved one, what would be the worst thing that would happen?

_____

_____

_____

BOOM!

LOVED ONE'S REACTIONS

1. How they may react:

Family members or friends may react in multiple different ways. For example:

- It's more than likely they'll react with kindness, asking how they can help and support you. As I mentioned, if you live with the chosen loved one you're planning to tell, then they're probably already aware and have suspected or known about your bulimia for a while. Maybe they've tried to approach you about it only not to be heard.
- They could react defensively; they may worry about how this news could be viewed within the family and that somebody might blame them. If this happens, point them to the internet. There's so much information floating on there. Over time and with knowledge, this sort of reaction often develops into a supportive role.
- Another reaction could be "just pull yourself together," whereby they don't know how to react or what to say to you. I know it's not what you want to hear, but educate them. Guide them toward researching bulimia for further resources to help them understand what you're going through. Giving them a copy of *Bulimia Sucks!* would be a great start, and with knowledge and understanding, they'll begin to open up to how to support you.

If they still don't react kindly or don't believe you, then maybe they aren't the right person to tell. So, perhaps, you could think of someone else, such as a trusted pastor, counselor, or best friend, to tell. But don't let this put you off, as most people will react with love and kindness.

2. Is it now time to 'Blurt... that... Hurt?

How to tell your loved one:

- This could be in person, on the phone, text, email, or messaging online. What would be the most comfortable for you?
- Write down what you want to say to them.
  Tell them your thoughts and feelings connected to your eating.
  What could they do to support you in reaching out for further help? If it makes it easier, practice what you're going to say.

Now make your own list of what you'll say to them.

_____

_____

_____

_____

STEP 10

Empowering Top Tips to Guide You Further in Your Recovery

"To be yourself in a world that is constantly trying to make you something else is the greatest accomplishment"

TABLE 37: ONE WISH TO FREEDOM
TABLE 38: GOALS
TABLE 39: POWERFUL POSITIVE GOALS
TABLE 40: ACTION PLAN
EXERCISE: TECHNIQUE TIME PRACTICE PLAN
TABLE 41: TECHNIQUE DAILY RECORD
TABLE 42: RECOVERY PATH

ONE WISH TO FREEDOM

What would be the one magical wish that will give you the courage, motivation, and inspiration to change and take that first step to freedom from bulimia?

Complete the ONE WISH TO FREEDOM table and answer these questions:

TABLE 37: ONE WISH TO FREEDOM

ASK YOURSELF:	YOUR ANSWERS:
What would that wish be?	
What's stopping you?	
What techniques can you use to reduce the blockages that are stopping you from starting?	List the specific techniques

ROLL WITH THE CONTROLS AND IGNITE YOUR GOALS

Recovery can be scary and not easy, so it's incredibly important to set goals for yourself. Setting clear, detailed, and achievable goals will help you to transform your thoughts into reality.

The more specific you can be when making your goals, the more powerful they become.

Complete TABLE 38: SPECIFIC GOALS and use that ancient art of 'writing' to list your specific goals in as much detail as possible.

TABLE 38: SPECIFIC GOALS

YOUR SPECIFIC GOALS
1.
2.
3.
4.
5.
6.
7.
8.
9.
10.

POWERFUL POSITIVE GOALS

So now you have your list of 10 goals you would like to achieve. To break this down further, choose 3 of these goals and solely focus on achieving these for the next week.

So, list in the Powerful Positive Goals Table your 3 main goals. In your answers, be as specific as you can, breaking it down to the first steps of how you'll achieve this.

Review this each week and change your goals.

TABLE 39: POWERFUL POSITIVE GOALS TABLE

YOUR POWERFUL POSITIVE GOAL	WHAT YOU CAN DO DIFFERENTLY TO ACHIEVE THIS
1.	
2.	
3.	

Repeat, repeat, repeat

The power comes from repetition. Keep repeating your new skills and goals to get what you want. Through repetition, your new skill can become a new habit and make a profound and lasting impact on you and your future.

RECOVERY ACTION PLAN

Arrrharrrr, you have come this far, and it's now time to gather all you've learned and decide how you're going to take this forward with an action plan.

In the Recovery Action Plan Table below, complete what you specifically need to change and then what you're going to do differently to help you make your action plan.

Complete the table of your action plan and answer the questions:

TABLE 40: RECOVERY ACTION PLAN

WHAT SPECIFICALLY DO I NEED TO CHANGE?	WHAT AM I GOING TO DO DIFFERENTLY?
1.	
2.	
3.	
4.	
5.	
6.	
7.	
8.	
9.	
10.	

TECHNIQUE TIME PRACTICE PLAN

Below is a table of all the incredible techniques you've learned in the book. I want you to work your way again through these. List the changes you need to make and find which techniques really fire up that motivation or help you change the way you feel. Then keep practicing these on a never-ending loop.

EXERCISE: TECHNIQUE TIME PRACTICE PLAN

TECHNIQUES	✓	CHECK WHICH ONES YOU'RE GOING TO BEGIN TO USE AND THEN LIST THE CHANGES YOU'RE GOING TO MAKE That is, what specific/ issue area are you going to work on?
"A NEW YOU"		
"SHRINK & BLINK"		
"INSTANT TRIGGER CHANGE"		
"ELECTRIFY YOUR MOTIVATION"		
"URGE SURFING"		
"CHANGE YOUR BELIEFS INSTANTLY"		
"THOUGHT STOPPING"		
"SPIN & WIN"		
"SHATTER THAT HABIT"		
"EFT"		
"INSPIRE YOUR SMOLDERING FIRE"		
"MOTIVATION BOOSTER"		

TECHNIQUES DAILY RECORD

Bonus Exercise

Now you have your list of which techniques you prefer. List which ones over the next week you're going to begin using, then adapt this over the coming weeks.

At the end of the workbook is a link to a downloadable PDF to print out and complete weekly.

TABLE 41: TECHNIQUES DAILY RECORD

MONDAY List which techniques to practice?	TUESDAY List which techniques to practice?	WEDNESDAY List which techniques to practice?	THURSDAY List which techniques to practice?	FRIDAY List which techniques to practice?	SATURDAY List which techniques to practice?	SUNDAY List which techniques to practice?
For Example: Spend 20 minutes working with the "Change Your Beliefs Instantly" technique	Start to learn urge surfing	Step into the "New You" technique four times today	Tap for 20 minutes on all my scared feelings	Learn and start to use the 'Shrink & Blink" technique	Start to work through my list of triggers with the "Instant Trigger Change" technique	Spend 15 minutes working with the "Spin and Win" technique to change any difficult feelings

RECOVERY PATH

What's going to motivate you to begin your action steps to recover from bulimia? What's more important to you than your bulimia? What's your life's goal?

Could it be?

1. That strong desire to be in a secure relationship and begin a family?
2. The final realization that yes, you would like to begin to build your career or your own company?
3. Enough is enough. It's time for you to have some fun in your life. Maybe to plan on traveling, enjoying the outdoors or learning a new sport?

What are your reasons for choosing to recover?

If you're ready NOW to begin on your recovery path, it's time to complete the table of your recovery path and answer this question, then make your list of powerful reasons why you want to change:

TABLE 42: RECOVERY PATH

WHAT ARE THE FIRST CHANGES YOU NEED TO MAKE?	REASONS WHY YOU WANT TO CHANGE
1.	
2.	
3.	
4.	
5.	
6.	
7.	
8.	
9.	
10.	

BOOM!

"Forgiveness and letting go are steps on our road back to happiness" TIAN DAYTON

FINALLY

Your recovery is all about you and you and you! You're the number one priority in your life now. You deserve to recover. Bulimia can be extremely demanding, isolating, and manipulative, but you're worth it wherever you are in your recovery.

In recovery, everyone is different, and the length of time it takes you to recover is perfect for you as long as you stay focused and achieve recovery. Think now about how taking these 10 steps will benefit not only you but also your family, friends, and people you don't even like! They'll all benefit.

The incredible strength, bravery, and pure mental motivation to stay focused on your recovery path is an extraordinary power you have within you. With the right tools, techniques, help, and support, you can do this.

It will be the most rewarding, life-changing, and incredible journey you'll ever go on.

You deserve freedom from bulimia

You deserve your recovery

And

You deserve to live.

RECOVERED – THIS IS WHO YOU WERE MEANT TO BE.

CONCLUSION

So, you've just finished reading this book and your mind is whirling with ideas of how to take yourself forward further, I suggest you begin by measuring where you are in your journey toward full recovery. Then go back to the beginning of your workbook, and reread through:

What worked for you?

What have you learned?

What else could you learn from the many different techniques, tables, and exercises?

Take each technique or table or learning and work on that with self-discipline until you're 100% sure you've either:

- learned the technique thoroughly and are enjoying the fruits of your labor
- completed the table thoroughly and are sure you've learned and benefited from it
- completed the exercise and understood what has come forth and are feeling more positive

How fired up and motivated are you to delve into and really focus on all the positive changes you could make right now?

Whether you're feeling fired up and motivated to continue changing your behaviors or feeling unsure of the changes possible. Address your thoughts and feelings and use the techniques to begin to change how you're feeling positively.

As you know, at the end of the workbook are links to techniques and video demonstrations. Included within this list are two powerful motivational techniques to fire and inspire you. So, zip to the techniques page and learn two empowering, inspirational tools to encourage your positive changes called:

"Electrify Your Motivation"

"Motivation Booster"

The more experience you gain by following the techniques, tables, and exercises, the more prepared you're going to be for difficult thoughts and feelings that may come up.

Just remember that you truly deserve to recover. It may not be an easy path, but it will be so worth it. Any step is a step closer to your end goal of your deserved happiness free from bulimia.

RECOVERED – THIS IS WHO YOU WERE MEANT TO BE.

VIDEO DEMONSTRATION LINKS AND INSTRUCTION STEPS FOR EACH TECHNIQUE

STEP 1

"A NEW YOU" TECHNIQUE

Video Demonstration Link: https://bulimiasucks.com/a-new-you/
PDF Instruction steps: https://bulimiasucks.com/the-new-you-technique-1/

STEP 2

"ELECTRIFY YOUR MOTIVATION" TECHNIQUE

Video Demonstration Link: https://bulimiasucks.com/electrify-your-motivation/
PDF Instruction steps: https://bulimiasucks.com/electrify-your-motivation-technique/

"SHRINK & BLINK" TECHNIQUE

Video Demonstration Link: https://bulimiasucks.com/shrink-blink/
PDF Instruction steps: https://bulimiasucks.com/shrink-and-blink-technique/

"INSTANT TRIGGER CHANGE" TECHNIQUE

Video Demonstration Link: http://bulimiasucks.com/instant-trigger-change/
PDF Instruction steps: https://bulimiasucks.com/the-instant-trigger-change-technique/

STEP 3

"URGE SURFING" TECHNIQUE

Video Demonstration Link: https://bulimiasucks.com/urge-surfing/
PDF Instruction steps: https://bulimiasucks.com/urge-surfing-technique/

STEP 4

PFD TABLE 13: STRUCTURED EATING PROGRAM PLAN
PDF print out: https://bulimiasucks.com/structured-eating-program-plan/

PFD TABLE 14: STRUCTURED EATING PROGRAM WEEKLY DIARY
PDF print out: https://bulimiasucks.com/structured-eating-program-weekly-diary/

STEP 5

"CHANGE YOUR BELIEFS INSTANTLY" TECHNIQUE
Video Demonstration Link: https://bulimiasucks.com/change-your-beliefs-instantly/
PDF Instruction steps: https://bulimiasucks.com/change-your-beliefs-instantly-technique/

"THOUGHT STOPPING" TECHNIQUE
This is a cool and powerful technique to help you work with any negative thoughts that come up. Check it out. It's super influential in freeing your mind of complicated thoughts.
Video Demonstration Link: https://bulimiasucks.com/thought-stopping/
PDF Instruction steps: https://bulimiasucks.com/thought-stopping-technique/

STEP 6

"SPIN & WIN" TECHNIQUE
Video Demonstration Link: https://bulimiasucks.com/spin-win/
PDF Instruction steps: https://bulimiasucks.com/spin-and-win-technique/

STEP 7

"SHATTER THAT HABIT" TECHNIQUE
Video Demonstration Link: https://bulimiasucks.com/shatter-that-habit/
PDF Instruction steps: https://bulimiasucks.com/shatter-that-habit-technique/

STEP 8

"EMOTIONAL FREEDOM TECHNIQUE"
Video Demonstration Link: https://bulimiasucks.com/emotional-freedom-technique/
PDF Instruction steps: https://bulimiasucks.com/emotional-freedom-technique/

STEP 9

"INSPIRE YOUR SMOLDERING FIRE" TECHNIQUE

Video Demonstration Link: https://bulimiasucks.com/inspire-your-smoldering-fire/

PDF Instruction steps: https://bulimiasucks.com/inspire-your-smoldering-fire-technique/

STEP 10

PFD TABLE 41: TECHNIQUES DAILY RECORD

PDF print out: https://bulimiasucks.com/techniques-daily-record/

"MOTIVATION BOOSTER" TECHNIQUE

Video Demonstration Link: https://bulimiasucks.com/motivation-booster/

PDF Instruction steps https://bulimiasucks.com/motivation-booster-technique/

Need more help through your recovery?

HOW TO CONTACT ME:

Bulimia can be excruciatingly isolating, and it can be inspiring to connect with others who are going through the same experiences as you. Also, you can hear how others have overcome particular problems in their recovery. So, come and join us on our Facebook page: https://www.facebook.com/groups/BulimiaSuck

Check out my websites:

https://katehudson-hall.com/

https://bulimiasucks.com/

Email me at:

katehudsonhall@gmail.com

I see clients on a one-to-one basis either in person or online via Skype, What's App, Facetime, and other web-based services.

"Small steps in the right direction can turn out to be the biggest step of your life"

ABOUT KATE HUDSON-HALL

At the age of 18, Kate began her bulimic career in earnest. Fifteen years later and after much help, she eventually freed herself from the clutches of anorexia and bulimia. Kate then stepped out and decided to take a different bulimic pathway. Feeling the great need to help others as she had been helped, she then trained as a psychotherapist, hypnotherapist, and NLP practitioner.

Having spent the last two decades working as an eating disorder therapist and wanting to reach out further than just her immediate clientele, Kate decided to write *Bulimia Sucks!* and now *Bulimia Sucks! Personal Workbook*, pouring all she has learned and experienced into helping others with eating disorders.

Kate lives and works in London and occasionally escapes to spend summers enjoying the views from the middle of a field on her land in Cornwall, overlooking the Atlantic Ocean.

Kate once spoke to the Queen on the telephone, by accident, who wanted to know if she was 'The General Public'… she had to come clean… and admit it!

REFERENCES

Bandler, R. (20_0). *Get the life you want.* HarperElement

Bandler, R., Roberti, A, & Fitzpatrick, O. (2013). *The ultimate introduction to NLP: How to build a successful life.* HarperCollins

Craig, G., & Craig, T. (n.d.). How to do the EFT tapping basics - The basic recipe. https://www.emofree.com/nl/eft-tutorial/tapping-basics/how-to-do-eft.html

Mayo Clinic. (n.d.) Bulimia: Overview. https://www.mayoclinic.org/diseases-conditions/bulimia/symptoms-causes/syc-20353615

Other Books by
Kate Hudson-Hall

Bulimia Sucks!

10 Simple Steps to Stop Bingeing and Purging

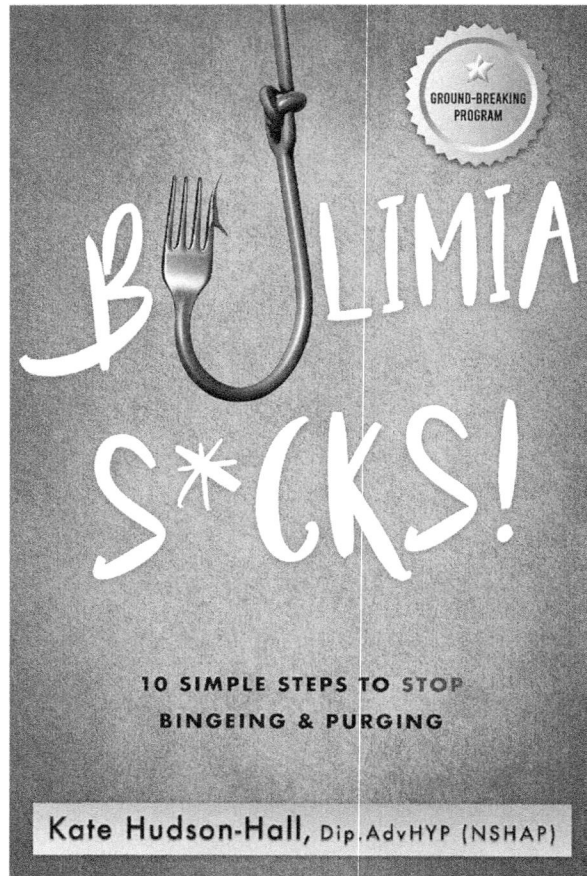

Available in print, eBook.

To grab your copy, go to: http://www.amazon.com/dp/B08RCPGNQW/

Coming soon:

Bulimia Sucks! The Audiobook

Bulimia Sucks! Personal Food Journal

ACKNOWLEDGMENTS

I would like to dedicate this book to all of the incredible people who have inspired me to write this personal workbook, especially:

Allan for always being there and supporting me with my eccentric ideas

The three musketeers, my sons, Luca, Tino and Lorenzo who have endured the waffle and reveled in the peace! Plus, my golden treasure, my granddaughter Lila Rose who is super enthusiastic Kiki, is writing another book

Judith, for her unbelievable wealth of support and incredible intuitive inspiration

Colleen, for her motivation, zealousness and her nourishment of encouragement

Louise, for her inspiration and her meticulous eye for perfection

My Goddaughter Kate for incredible artistic talents

Cousin Karen for her belief in me and her immense support

Gil for her encouragement and free-flowing wisdom

For all his help, advice, guidance, and wealth of knowledge, my editor Wayne Purdin plus for not telling me this is a load of balderdash!

And finally, for those with bulimia, stay focused on your pathway to freedom. AND because you CAN do this.

"REMEMBER TO DOWNLOAD YOUR

BONUS FREEBIE"

As a huge thank you, I have created a

CALMING MP3 RELAXATION DOWNLOAD

When you feel overwhelmed by life's stress, this relaxation recording will help calm and relax you.

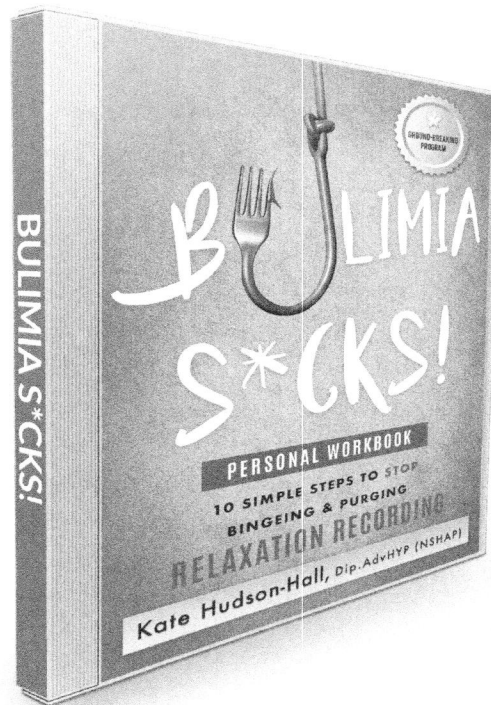

CLICK HERE TO DOWNLOAD:

https://bulimiasucks.com/bulimia-sucks-workbook-relaxation-recording-mp3/

Can You Help?

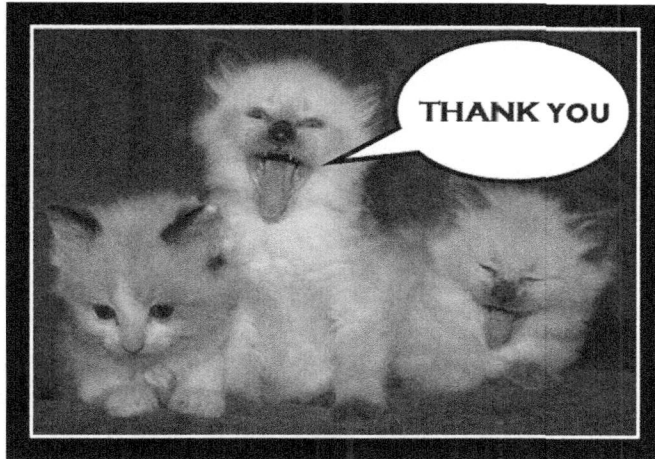

Thank You for Reading My Book!

I really appreciate all of your feedback, and I love hearing what you have to say.

So, I need your input to make the next version of this book and my future books even more empowering.

This will not only help others to begin to break their bulimic behaviors but be incredibly rewarding for me to know how you've benefited from following the steps.

This way, you can help empower others in the way this personal workbook has empowered you.

Please leave me an honest review on Amazon; yes, I would love to know what you thought of the workbook.

Thank you so much!

Kate (Also known as 'The General Public.')

Printed in Great Britain
by Amazon

23284369R00077